PRAISE FOR *WINTER FIRE*

Drawing from the bottomless well of Chesterton's poetry and prose, Ryan Whitaker Smith renews and refreshes us with these tidings of comfort and joy.

DALE AHLQUIST
President, Society of Gilbert Keith Chesterton

In this beautifully designed and illustrated book, Ryan Whitaker Smith serves up a feast of G. K. Chesterton's wit and wisdom for Christmas. Even more, in the devotional reflections, Ryan builds on Chesterton's work with memorable expression and striking insight of his own. A holiday treat!

TREVIN WAX
Author of *The Thrill of Orthodoxy* and an annotated version of Chesterton's *Orthodoxy* with guided reading

Some books are keepsakes because of their colorful presentation, some because of the content they present, and some like *Winter Fire* because of both. Smith's seasonal collection is brilliant, and convincing that the prolific Chesterton doesn't just write a lot of things, but a lot of important things.

JERRY PATTENGALE
Founding scholar, Museum of the Bible (DC); University Professor, Indiana Wesleyan University; author, *The New Book of Christian Martyrs*

Lavishly illustrated and brimming with wisdom and whimsy, Ryan Whitaker Smith gives us a lovely Christmas book to be enjoyed by young and old alike throughout the year. Here delightful stories, excerpts, and reflective exercises are jeweled with poems, recipes, traditions, and even games! The charm of a time past illuminates the gift of our Savior ever into our present—in a manner of which Chesterton would have approved. For, in the words of C. S. Lewis, "Is any pleasure on earth as great as a circle of Christian friends by a good [winter] fire?"

CAROLYN WEBER
Professor at New College Franklin, and award-winning author of *Surprised by Oxford*, now a feature film

A Merry Christmas

WINTER FIRE

CHRISTMAS WITH G. K. CHESTERTON

RYAN WHITAKER SMITH

MOODY PUBLISHERS

CHICAGO

Published in association with the literary agency of WTA Media in Franklin, Tennessee.

Edited by Connor Sterchi
Cover design and illustration: Stephen Crotts
Cover and interior design and art direction: Erik M. Peterson

Library of Congress Cataloging-in-Publication Data

Names: Smith, Ryan Whitaker, 1983- author.
Title: Winter fire : Christmas with G. K. Chesterton / Ryan Whitaker Smith.
Description: Chicago : Moody Publishers, [2023] | Includes bibliographical
   references and index. | Summary: Experience the warmth of Christmas through
   the winsome wit and wisdom of beloved writer G. K. Chesterton. This
   devotional - perfect for the Christmas season - includes selections of
   Chesterton's writings, accompanied with commentary, Scripture readings,
   and reflections. Be encouraged by Chesterton's insight, charmed by the
   Victorian-inspired artwork, and delighted by the traditional English
   recipes. Make Chesterton's poetry, short stories, and essays a part of
   your Christmas tradition! A festive celebration of childlike wonder, the
   beautifully illustrated Winter Fire is a unique and meaningful gift"--
   Provided by publisher.
Identifiers: LCCN 2023000383 (print) | LCCN 2023000384 (ebook) | ISBN
   9780802429285 (hardcover) | ISBN 9780802473868 (ebook)
Subjects: LCSH: Christmas--Devotional literature. | Christmas--Literary
   collections. | Chesterton, G. K. (Gilbert Keith), 1874-1936--Criticism
   and interpretation. | BISAC: RELIGION / Holidays / Christmas & Advent |
   RELIGION / Christian Living / Devotional
Classification: LCC BV45 .S489 2023 (print) | LCC BV45 (ebook) | DDC
   242/.335--dc23/eng/20230309
LC record available at https://lccn.loc.gov/2023000383
LC ebook record available at https://lccn.loc.gov/2023000384

Originally delivered by fleets of horse-drawn wagons, the affordable paperbacks from D. L. Moody's publishing house resourced the church and served everyday people. Now, after more than 125 years of publishing and ministry, Moody Publishers' mission remains the same—even if our delivery systems have changed a bit. For more information on other books (and resources) created from a biblical perspective, go to www.moodypublishers.com or write to:

Moody Publishers
820 N. LaSalle Boulevard
Chicago, IL 60610

1 3 5 7 9 10 8 6 4 2

Printed in the United States of America

CONTENTS

GAMES & TRADITIONS

INTRODUCTION

G. K. Chesterton, one of the most prolific writers of the twentieth century, wrote more in his lifetime than most people get around to reading in theirs. He wrote so broadly, in so many contexts and genres, that it seems as if, at some point or other, he touched on virtually every subject one could possibly think to write about. He was a novelist, a journalist, a historian, a playwright, a lay theologian, a Christian apologist. He published nearly a hundred books, thousands of essays, a handful of plays, and several hundred poems. A staple of the literary scene in London in the late nineteenth and early twentieth centuries, he was a larger-than-life figure in more ways than one: his intelligence was formidable. His wit, inimitable. His girth, remarkable.

I first encountered Chesterton's writing as a teenager, when his novel *The Man Who Was Thursday* was assigned as required reading for an English class. I don't recall it having much of an impact on me at the time, if I did indeed read it in its entirety. A few years later, by what I now consider to be a stroke of divine providence, I stumbled upon a volume of Chesterton's Father Brown stories collecting dust on my shelf and decided, for whatever reason, to give them a go (I have a habit of buying books on impulse, with the sincere intention of one day getting around to reading them. Results vary, but my library continues to grow). I was struck not just by the lucidity of the prose, or its witty inventiveness, but by something

latent beneath the surface of those cleverly constructed stories fea-
turing Chesterton's bumbling-but-brilliant detective priest: they
were beautifully written and utterly delightful, but they were also
wise and *good*—not merely entertaining, but somehow *formative*. It
would be disingenuous to say that I found Father Brown that day; it
was more like he found me.

In short order, I went on to consume *Orthodoxy, The Everlasting
Man, The Napoleon of Notting Hill, The Flying Inn, The Ball and the
Cross, The Ballad of the White Horse*, a fresh read of *The Man Who
Was Thursday*, as well as several others. I've now been journeying
with Chesterton for fifteen years or so, and I'm still making my way
through his astonishing body of work. Because of his extraordinary
prolificacy, he is a gift that keeps on giving. Nearly a hundred years
after his passing, his words continue to resonate with brilliance,
wisdom, and wit. His pseudo-theological works like *Orthodoxy* and
The Everlasting Man (which, in C. S. Lewis's words, "baptized his
intellect"[1]) have influenced Christians around the world (though
he famously converted to Catholicism later in his life and remained
an ardent defender of the Roman Catholic Church until the day he
died, he is the rare Catholic writer with broad readership among
Catholics and Protestants alike).

His Father Brown stories are not just popular in their own right,
but have inspired one of the most successful and longest-running
BBC shows of the modern era, starring the delightful Mark Williams,
whom I was fortunate enough to work with on my film *Surprised
by Oxford*. As I write these words, I am in the early stages of pre-
production on a film based on Chesterton's novel *The Ball and the
Cross*. It excites me to imagine how it might, alongside an effort such
as this book, introduce yet more people to this delightful mentor I've
been journeying with for all these years.

So, why a book based specifically on his writings about Christmas?
First, Chesterton was enthusiastic about his love of Christmas and

wrote voluminously about the subject. In fact, this is not the first book to collect some of these writings. *The Spirit of Christmas*, edited by Marie Smith (now out of print), was released in the 1980s and is a cherished title by Chesterton fans. Much of the same content appears in this book, but I've taken a different approach to the material. Here, excerpts of Chesterton's writing are presented in a devotional format as daily readings, alongside my commentary, Scripture passages, and reflection questions—but that barely scratches the surface of what is contained in this volume. The devotional readings make up roughly the first half of *Winter Fire*, while the second half is a compendium of poems, essays, short stories, recipes, and more. In addition to the quotes that are the basis of the devotions, there are many more scattered throughout the book and embedded within my commentary.

There is no doubt in my mind that this is the most comprehensive collection of Chesterton's writings on Christmas ever published—a statement I make with utter humility, because it is not, in any way, exhaustive. Before embarking on this project, I was familiar with much of the material that would find its way into this book, but my research revealed an embarrassment of riches in that department. I knew Chesterton wrote a lot about Christmas; frankly, I didn't know he wrote *that* much. I've done my best to fit in as much as possible without overwhelming the reader. I'm aware that for many, this book will serve as an introduction to Chesterton, and I've tried to keep that in mind. On that note, a word of advice: Chesterton's writing can be an acquired taste. If necessary, read his words slowly, in order to take in all that he's saying (often he's saying several things at once).

Second, it's not just that Chesterton has a lot to say about Christmas; he has something *important* to say. With his virtuosic flair, he eloquently (and often humorously) points us back to the true meaning of Christmas. He revels in the festive traditions of Christmas. He challenges the modern opposition to Christmas. At a time when

Christmas is becoming increasingly commercialized and detached from its Christian origins, Chesterton's words seem more relevant than ever before.

Lastly, a word about the title, which is taken from a quote featured in the reading for Day 13: "Christ is not merely a summer sun of the prosperous but a winter fire for the unfortunate."[2] The image of a fire burning amid the frosts of winter seemed a fitting image to draw from for a book that not only celebrates the comfort, joy, and revelry of Christmas, but the mercy of God who has called us to His everlasting feast.

A WORD OF INSTRUCTION

The season of Advent, as traditionally observed by the church, is around twenty-five days, beginning at the end of November and ending on December 24 (the four weeks leading up to Christmas). As Chesterton will point out in the pages to come, despite the modern tendency to treat Christmas as a one-day celebration, it is, in fact, a feast lasting for twelve days, beginning on December 25 and ending on January 5.

Though Chesterton does occasionally touch on Advent specifically, he often speaks of Christmas in a more general sense, so rather than arranging the daily readings in the first half of this book into Advent and Christmas categories, I've provided thirty entries total. How you decide to incorporate these into your holiday season is ultimately up to you, but I will offer a few suggestions:

- You can, of course, begin on December 1. In this case, you will get through the devotional readings by December 30.

- Or, if you choose to begin on the first Sunday of Advent, the readings will take you through roughly Christmas Day or late December, depending on the year.

- My recommendation would be to go through the daily readings during Advent and explore the additional content in the back half of the book throughout the twelve days of Christmas—but that is merely a friendly suggestion.

Whatever your approach, the intended purpose of the supplemental material is to provide content to explore at your own pace during the holiday season.

DAILY READINGS

ᗩᗨ DAY 1 ᗢᗣ

AN INVITATION TO WALK BACKWARDS THROUGH HISTORY

It was in the season of Christmas that I came out of my little garden in that "field of the beeches" between the Chilterns and the Thames, and began to walk backwards through history to the place from which Christmas came.

THE NEW JERUSALEM (1920)[1]

So begins *The New Jerusalem*, G. K. Chesterton's travelogue chronicling his journey to the Holy Land. But before the destination, there is the journey. For Chesterton, it begins in a backyard in Beaconsfield, England, as the large, mustached man unlatches the garden gate and sets off on his adventure. Perhaps yours begins in a kitchen, with a strong cup of black coffee, or in a comfortable corner of the living room, the windows limned with frost. For me, it begins in a home office I affectionately call "the library," as the fields around my house are blanketed with early morning fog. Regardless of our various points of departure, this book is an invitation to link arms

15

and set off together, as we "walk backwards through history to the place from which Christmas came."

Is our celebration of Christmas not an attempt to do this very thing? Is the memorializing of an event not an effort, at some level, to relive it? Our traditions and ceremonies, rituals and feast days, are the inner workings of a psychological and emotional time machine. To sing "while shepherds watched their flocks at night" is to hum an incantation that might, if we allow it, transport us to a grassy hillside in Judea two thousand years ago, when celestial choirs filled the sky and proclaimed good news for all mankind. A box swathed in paper and ribbon is a talisman with the power to spirit us away to a humble home in first-century Palestine, at the moment when visitors from the East arrive, arms laden with gifts, eyes wide with wonder. In celebrating Christmas, we long, in some sense, to be one with it—to enter the story ourselves.

It would behoove us to remember that, as the journey precedes the destination, the season of Advent precedes Christmas. Advent, as observed by Christians for millennia, is a time of expectant wait-ing, an observance of a time when Israel's prophets were as silent as their God and their people yearned for a promised (and much delayed) deliverer. As the famous hymn pleads, "O come, O come, Emmanuel, and ransom captive Israel . . ." Advent is a desire in the Now for the Not Yet. In the coming days, we will further explore the traditional observance of Advent and Christmas and how we might recover those customs in our modern, distracted age.

Think of this book as a travelogue into the heart of Christmas, with the tall, heavyset man as our trusted guide. Let us keep our ears (and hearts) open, for I believe he has much to say to us along the way (he's loquacious, six feet four inches tall, and nearly three hundred pounds, so he's somewhat difficult to ignore). In speaking of travel, Chesterton once wrote,

I cannot see any Battersea here; I cannot see any London or any England. I cannot see that door. I cannot see that chair: because a cloud of sleep and custom has come across my eyes. The only way to get back to them is to go somewhere else; and that is the real object of travel and the real pleasure of holidays. Do you suppose that I go to France in order to see France? Do you suppose that I go to Germany in order to see Germany? I shall enjoy them both; but it is not them that I am seeking. I am seeking Battersea. The whole object of travel is not to set foot on foreign land; it is at last to set foot on one's own country as a foreign land.[2]

The purpose of our journey is not so much to dwell in "the place from which Christmas came," but to allow that place to dwell *in us*, to return to our own country with christened eyes, to look upon our everyday surroundings with a baptized imagination.

As we exit the garden and turn the corner, the large man's cane clinking along the cobblestones, he mutters under his breath, "Christmas belongs to an order of ideas which never really perished, and which is now less likely to perish than ever." Just then, he is momentarily stunned into silence by the image of a sparrowcock perched upon the branch of a tall, barren tree, silhouetted against the darkening sky. "It had from the first a sort of glamour of a lost cause," he says with a twinkle in his eye. "It was like an everlasting sunset. It is only the things that never die that get the reputation of dying."[3]

With that, he turns and continues down the street. We hasten to follow, as the first flurries of snow begin to fall . . .

SCRIPTURE READING & REFLECTION

Behold, the days are coming, declares the LORD, when I will fulfill the promise I made to the house of Israel and the house of Judah. In those days and at that time I will cause a righteous Branch to spring up for David, and he shall execute justice and righteousness in the land. In those days Judah will be saved, and Jerusalem will dwell securely. And this is the name by which it will be called: "The LORD is our righteousness."

JEREMIAH 33:14-16

How might you prepare space in your heart for Christ during this season?

How can you make time for silence and contemplation in the midst of an increasingly busy time of year?

Meditate on some long journeys in your life, when the promise of deliverance seemed far away. Reflect on the mercies of God that were with you in the midst of your "expectant waiting."

⚓ DAY 2 ⚓

A WARNING TO THOSE IN DANGER OF CELEBRATING CHRISTMAS PREMATURELY

All the old wholesome customs in connection with Christmas were to the effect that one should not touch or see or know or speak of something before the actual coming of Christmas Day. Thus, for instance, children were never given their presents until the actual coming of the appointed hour. The presents were kept tied up in brown-paper parcels, out of which an arm of a doll or the leg of a donkey sometimes accidentally stuck. I wish this principle were adopted in respect of modern Christmas ceremonies and publications. The editors of the magazines bring out their Christmas numbers so long before the time that the reader is more likely to be lamenting for the turkey of last year than to have seriously settled down to a solid anticipation of the turkey which is to come. Christmas numbers of magazines ought to be tied up in brown paper and kept for Christmas Day. On consideration, I should favor the editors being tied up in brown paper. Whether the leg or arm of an editor should ever be allowed to protrude I leave to individual choice.

THE ILLUSTRATED LONDON NEWS (1906)[1]

The celebration of Christmas, as traditionally observed by the church, does not, in fact, conclude on December 25. Christmas Day is but the beginning of twelve days of festive celebration (as expressed in the well-known carol "The Twelve Days of Christmas"). That certain ceremonies and publications in Chesterton's day were rushing to celebrate Christmas prematurely betrayed a fundamental misunderstanding of the Advent and Christmas traditions. As he says elsewhere,

> Modern men have a vague feeling that when they have come to the feast, they have come to the finish. By modern commercial customs, the preparations for it have been so very long and the practice of it seems so very short.[2]

If this sounds familiar, perhaps it's because we tend to observe Christmas in the following fashion: Immediately after Thanksgiving in America, radio stations begin playing Christmas music. TV networks begin airing Christmas movies. Families begin stringing up decorations. The so-called Christmas season (a somewhat vague designation) is officially initiated. Festivities continue through December 25 (the day when families gather and gifts are exchanged), after which decorations are unceremoniously stripped away, trees are dragged to the curb to be hauled off with the trash, news anchors recap the holiday in past-tense language, talking about how Christmas *was*, how it *went*, what *happened*. In the days following Christmas Day, a general malaise hangs in the air, like dissipating smoke from a fireworks display. Christmas came and went, in grand but short-lived fashion.

Whatever it was, whatever it was for, it is now definitively and categorically over. "This is, of course, in sharp contrast to the older traditional customs, in the days when it was a sacred festival for a simpler people," Chesterton reminds us. "Then the preparation took the form of the more austere season of Advent and the fast of Christmas Eve. But when men passed on to the feast of Christmas, it went on for a long time after the feast of Christmas Day."[3]

The "austere" season of Advent, as we have established, is a time of expectant waiting. Christmas, fittingly, is its own season—a prolonged feast sustained for nearly two weeks. Chesterton reminds us that in the "old wholesome customs" Christmas would not be spoken of throughout the season of Advent. Gifts were kept wrapped until Christmas Day, when they would be opened at last—not all at once in a dizzying blur—but one at a time, over the course of twelve days (I would venture to say most people today lack the patience for such a thing). If this all sounds rather foreign to us, it's only further proof that the modern Westernized approach to Christmas has been ingrained in us from an early age. Thankfully, we serve a God who invites us to become like children, so there's always time to unlearn a few things.

The challenge I present to you is this: resist the urge to celebrate Christmas prematurely. Give Advent its proper due, armed with reverent patience and an expectant heart. When Christmas comes, celebrate with prolonged joy "in a crescendo of festivity until Twelfth Night"[4] (I'll leave the means of gift distribution up to you). Rebel against our modern culture by joining the ranks of the church, which outlasts all cultures. Or shall Chesterton tie you up in brown paper as well?

SCRIPTURE READING & REFLECTION

So then, brothers, stand firm and hold to the traditions that you were taught by us, either by our spoken word or by our letter.

2 THESSALONIANS 2:15

Consider how you might allow the traditions of the church to influence your celebration of Christmas this year.

Consider how you might "unlearn" some modern holiday traditions in favor of a more traditional observance of Advent and Christmas.

What would it take for you to sustain a "crescendo of festivity until Twelfth Night"?

~⚬ DAY 3 ⚬~

IN REGARD TO CERTAIN OBJECTIONS TO THE CELEBRATION OF CHRISTMAS

It is the greatest glory of the Christian tradition that it has
incorporated so many pagan traditions. But it is most glorious
of all, to my mind, when they are popular traditions. And
the best and most obvious example is the way in which
Christianity did incorporate, in so far as it did incorporate,
the old human and heathen conception of the Winter Feast.
There are, indeed, two profound and mysterious truths to
be balanced here. The first is that what was then heathen
was still human; that is, it was both mystical and material;
it expressed itself in sacred substances and sacramental acts;
it understood the mystery of trees and waters and the holy
flame. And the other, which will be a much more tactless
and irritating assertion, is that while a thing is heathen it
is not yet completely human. But the point here is that the
pagan element in Christmas came quite natural to Christians,
because it was not in fact very far from Christianity.

G.K.'S WEEKLY (1936)[1]

Though it might come as a surprise to those of us who celebrate Christmas with gleeful abandon (present company included), many Christians throughout the world, including those from the Quaker and Seventh Day Adventist traditions, choose not to celebrate Christmas at all. Though Chesterton once went so far as to say that "the man who does not keep Christmas is an incomplete human being,"[2] perhaps we might preserve an ounce of understanding for those who happen to possess a different opinion on the subject. That being said, the objection that Christmas is merely a Christian "spin" on a pagan holiday, that our Christmas traditions are inherited from pagan traditions, that there is nothing inherently Christian about Christmas—is a topic worthy of discussion.

For Chesterton, the fact that Christmas might indeed have borrowed something from the dark ages of paganism was not a cause for concern, in and of itself. In fact, he was unequivocal in his preference for the pagan superstition of the ancient world over the rational skepticism of the modern one. Paganism, for its many faults, could not, after all, be accused (like modernity) of treating the world as a disenchanted place. At the very least, paganism recognized that the world is charged with meaning. It understood "the mystery of trees and waters and the holy flame." This is what he means when he says that paganism "was not in fact very far from Christianity." What he is implying, in so many words, is that it might be easier to make a Christian out of an idol-worshiping pagan than a secular humanist: that a Druid, well-versed in human sacrifice, might be closer to grasping the atoning death of Christ than a materialist with no framework for spirituality (then again, God makes even the impossible possible).

When Chesterton makes the claim that "the greatest glory of the Christian tradition is that it has incorporated so many pagan traditions" (a statement sure to throw fuel on the fire for those Christians convinced of the heathen darkness at the root of the holiday), he does not mean that Christmas should be viewed as pagan in spirit, but rather that it has *reframed* and *redeemed* certain pagan traditions with the light of the gospel. Though historians such as Tom Holland challenge the claim that the winter celebration of Christmas (and specifically the date of December 25) originated in paganism,[3] Christmas does share certain undeniable similarities with the aforementioned Winter Feast, not least of which the fact that it is a feast that takes place in winter.

But there is a deeper observation here. What Chesterton is implying is that the pagans had somehow "anticipated the supreme miracle"— a concept echoed in the writings of C. S. Lewis and J. R. R. Tolkien. After all, why should the redeeming work of Christ not extend to human traditions? If land soaked in the blood of heathen sacrifice could be reclaimed by the kingdom of God (as in the time of ancient Israel), why should feasts and festivals not be reclaimed? As Chesterton says, "It is no controversial point against the Christians that they felt they could take up and continue such traditions among the pagans; it only shows that the Christians knew a Christian thing when they saw it."[4]

As he wrote in an article published in 1901, "When a learned man tells me that on the 25th of December I am really astronomically worshipping the sun, I answer that I am not. I am practising a particular personal religion, the pleasures of which (right or wrong) are not in the least astronomical. If he says that the cult of Christmas and the cult of Apollo are the same, I answer that they are utterly different; and I ought to know, for I have held both of them. I believed in Apollo when I was quite little; and I believe in Christmas now that I am very, very big."[5] This season, let us attempt, however imperfectly, to join him—laying aside childish things while retaining the faith of a child. In the kingdom of God, it's the only way to grow "very, very big."

SCRIPTURE READING & REFLECTION

I became a minister according to the stewardship from God that was given to me for you, to make the word of God fully known, the mystery hidden for ages and generations but now revealed to his saints. To them God chose to make known how great among the Gentiles are the riches of the glory of this mystery, which is Christ in you, the hope of glory.

COLOSSIANS 1:25-27

Meditate on Paul's words—that Christ is "the mystery hidden for ages" and "the hope of glory." How does this connect to the idea of Christmas "redeeming" pagan traditions?

Reflect on your own life and consider some of the ways Christ has redeemed your past.

How might you practice Christ-centered hope during this season?

26

✧⊰ DAY 4 ⊱✧

OF PARADOXES, CELESTIAL LADDERS, AND MOVING WHEELS

> The exciting quality of Christmas rests on an ancient and
> admitted paradox. It rests upon the paradox that the power
> and center of the whole universe may be found in some
> seemingly small matter, that the stars in their courses may
> move like a moving wheel around the neglected outhouse
> of an inn.
>
> THE DAILY NEWS (1901)[1]

G. K. Chesterton was called "the prince of paradox" for good reason. With the skill of a diamond miner, he unearthed paradoxes at
every turn. He mused on contradictions, inconsistencies, and incon-
gruities. He reveled at irony, disparity, and absurdity. He spoke of a
God "as narrow as the universe."[2] Of a cross composed of conflicting
angles, opening its "arms to the four winds."[3] Of Christmas resting
"on an ancient and admitted paradox"—that the greatest gift the
world has ever received arrived in obscurity, in a backwater town

in ancient Palestine, on a night when the streets were filled with drunken laughter and the inns were full, and no one was in the mood for miracles. Only those actively looking for Christ's arrival might find Him, and then only if they squeezed past the crowds, zigzagged through back alleys and out into the cool dark, to a place where cattle noises threatened to muffle the sounds of a baby's cries.

Chesterton wisely recognized the profound irony of the incarnation, marveling that "the power and center of the whole universe may be found in some seemingly small matter"—that God Himself would choose to enter human history in the most anticlimactic fashion imaginable (perhaps God, for all His grandeur, has a sense of humor after all). As Chesterton says elsewhere, "Christmas is built upon a beautiful and intentional paradox; that the birth of the homeless should be celebrated in every home."[4]

Time and again throughout Scripture, God baffles us, perplexes us, bewilders us. He who inhabits eternity dwells with the humble and contrite of heart (Isa. 57:15). The celestial conductor of wind and earthquake and fire makes His presence known in a gentle whisper (1 Kings 19:12–13). The King of kings arrives not in a castle, but in "the neglected outhouse of an inn." God Himself is a glorious paradox. As Chesterton eloquently articulates in his poem "Gloria in Profundis":

> Outrushing the fall of man
> Is the height of the fall of God.[5]

There is a concept known in some cultures as an *axis mundi*, defined by *Merriam-Webster's Dictionary* as a "line or stem through the earth's center connecting its surface to the underworld and the heavens and around which the universe revolves."[6] In other words, it is a "thin place"—a place of unusually high spiritual energy, a place where heaven meets earth. Genesis 28 recounts the story of Jacob's dream, in which he saw "a ladder set up on the earth, and the top of it reached to heaven. And behold, the angels of God were ascending and descending on it!" (Gen. 28:12).

For those with the eyes to see, the cave in that forgotten corner of Bethlehem was (at least for a time) an *axis mundi*, "the stars in their courses" turning "like a moving wheel" around the humble birthplace of Christ, who is Himself the physical embodiment of the intersection of heaven and earth. When Nathanael declared that Jesus was, in fact, the Son of God, Jesus replied, "You will see heaven opened, and the angels of God ascending and descending on the Son of Man" (John 1:51). Jacob's ladder was a prophetic picture of Christ, "the mediator of a new covenant" (Heb. 9:15). Ephesians 1 tells us that the whole purpose of God's plan of redemption is to "unite all things in [Christ], things in heaven and things on earth" (v. 10).

As Chesterton says in *The Everlasting Man*,

> No other story, no pagan legend or philosophical anecdote or historical event, does in fact affect any of us with that peculiar and even poignant impression produced on us by the word Bethlehem. No other birth of a god or childhood of a sage seems to us to be Christmas or anything like Christmas. It is either too cold or too frivolous, or too formal and classical, or too simple and savage, or too occult and complicated. Not one of us, whatever his opinions, would ever go to such a scene with the sense that he was going home.[7]

There was no room in the inn for Mary and Joseph, when the universe itself could not house the child Mary carried in her womb. For a brief time, the humble cave was the resting place of He who is the eternal resting place of every humble heart. He who was born that night is He through whom all things were born. In the moving conclusion of Chesterton's poem "The House of Christmas," he writes:

To an open house in the evening
Home shall men come,
To an older place than Eden
And a taller town than Rome.
To the end of the way of the wandering star,
To the things that cannot be and that are,
To the place where God was homeless
And all men are at home.[8]

Let us join that holy pilgrimage and follow the star to the humble, paradoxical place where hope is born, where heaven and earth meet, where we are eternally at home.

SCRIPTURE READING & REFLECTION

For thus says the One who is high and lifted up,
who inhabits eternity, whose name is Holy:
"I dwell in the high and holy place,
and also with him who is of a contrite and lowly spirit,
to revive the spirit of the lowly,
and to revive the heart of the contrite."

ISAIAH 57:15

Why does God choose to side with the contrite and the lowly? How does this connect to Jesus' pronouncement that the pure in heart will "see God" (Matt. 5:8)?

Consider how this passage in Isaiah anticipates Christ's coming.

Consider how you might adopt a posture of humility and contriteness during this season.

⋰⋰ DAY 5 ⋱⋱

IN CELEBRATION OF
THE UTTER UNSUITABILITY
OF CHRISTMAS
TO THE MODERN WORLD

Christmas is utterly unsuited to the great future that is now
opening before us. Christmas is not founded on the great
communal conception which can only find its final expression
in Communism. Christmas does not really help the higher
and healthier and more vigorous expansion of Capitalism.
Christmas cannot be expected to fit in with modern hopes of
a great social future. Christmas is a contradiction of modern
thought. Christmas is an obstacle to modern progress. Rooted
in the past, and even the remote past, it cannot assist a world
in which the ignorance of history is the only clear evidence
of the knowledge of science. Born among miracles reported
from two thousand years ago, it cannot expect to impress that
sturdy common sense which can withstand the plainest and
most palpable evidence for miracles happening at this moment.

G.K.'S WEEKLY (1933)[1]

The future Chesterton speaks of is our present. Our world, in various ways, is the fulfillment of his grim vision: a world unmoored from tradition, set adrift on the ever-changing tide of fad and fashion (he reminds us elsewhere that "fallacies do not cease to be fallacies because they become fashions"[2]). Modern culture is infatuated with all that is shiny and new and noteworthy. Witness the cult of technology. Behold the ever-expanding elasticity of "expressive individualism." Watch as the masses pile onto every bandwagon promising truth and justice in the name of progress (marvel not when the wagon goes off a cliff). Puffed up with "chronological snobbery" (to borrow C. S. Lewis's phrase),[3] modernity peers over its shoulder with contempt on the ignorant, unenlightened ages of the past.

Chesterton poses the question: What place does Christmas have in a world such as ours? Blind adherence to science often requires the willful "ignorance of history." The "great communal conception" of Communism refuses to acknowledge the sacred individuality of human beings made in the image of God. The "healthier and more vigorous expansion of Capitalism" has little to gain from a holiday that values giving over receiving. The "social future" of tomorrow, promising peace and prosperity for all (so long as you ebb and flow with the changing societal tides), might go so far as to mock the humble beginnings of a tradition as selfless and unproductive as Christmas.

Though modern Western culture still carves out time for Christmas, "the holidays" have largely become crass and commercialized—a marriage of unbridled consumerism and vague humanitarianism, rather than a celebration of a Savior who came to save us from ourselves. As Chesterton once observed, "Moving step by step, in the majestic march of Progress, we have first vulgarised Christmas and then denounced it as vulgar. Christmas has become too commercial; so many of these thinkers would destroy the Christmas that has been spoiled, and preserve the commercialism that has spoiled it."[4]

If this all sounds rather bleak, I suggest that what makes Christmas "utterly unsuited" to the modern world is what makes it so worthy of recognition. Christmas is gloriously out of step with the times, for it outlasts the times. It champions obscurity over visibility. Humility over hubris. Divine mercy over human effort. Today, let us raise our glasses and our voices and our trees and our stockings in honor of the glorious unsuitability of Christmas. Let us savor the sheer irrationality of it. Shout with joy at the blatant absurdity of it. Like all that is of God, it is a blasphemy to the narcissist. An insult to the hedonist. A farce to the self-reliant and self-consumed. Hallelujah. Pour yourself another glass of sherry. Help yourself to another slice of cake. Praise God that that which was "born among miracles reported from two thousand years ago" still makes miracles in human hearts today (though the voices of this age "can withstand the plainest and most palpable evidence" of such a thing). Christmas is utterly unsuitable to the modern world, which makes it utterly indispensable to the church.

SCRIPTURE READING & REFLECTION

Where is the one who is wise? Where is the scribe? Where is the debater of this age? Has not God made foolish the wisdom of the world? For since, in the wisdom of God, the world did not know God through wisdom, it pleased God through the folly of what we preach to save those who believe. For Jews demand signs and Greeks seek wisdom, but we preach Christ crucified, a stumbling block to Jews and folly to Gentiles, but to those who are called, both Jews and Greeks, Christ the power of God and the wisdom of God. For the foolishness of God is wiser than men, and the weakness of God is stronger than men.

I CORINTHIANS 1:20-25

Consider Paul's words about "the foolishness of God being wiser than men" and "the weakness of God being stronger than men." How might this idea affect your observance of Advent and Christmas?

Think of some traditions you might incorporate this season that are "utterly unsuitable" to the modern world.

How might you resist the commercialization of Christmas this year?

ON CHRISTMAS
AS A LITMUS TEST
FOR SPIRITUAL BUOYANCY

> Most sensible people say that adults cannot be expected to
> appreciate Christmas as much as children appreciate it. But
> I am not sure that even sensible people are always right; and
> this has been my principal reason for deciding to be silly—a
> decision that is now irrevocable. It may be because I am silly,
> but I rather think that, relatively to the rest of the year, I
> enjoy Christmas more than I did when I was a child.
>
> THE ILLUSTRATED LONDON NEWS (1913)[1]

Chesterton touches on a great irony at the heart of the gospel.
How can one reach maturity while maintaining childlikeness?
How can one grow tall in grace while short in cynicism? How can
one "put away childish things" and yet retain the faith of a child? As
it turns out, Christmas is an excellent litmus test for spiritual buoy-
ancy. Ask yourself: *Do I enjoy Christmas as much or more than I did
when I was a child? Has my appreciation of Christmas diminished*

over time or grown exponentially as I have grown older? If not, then you might be one of the sensible people Chesterton is warning us about—those who have no time for fun and games, who believe that silliness is synonymous with youth. What he challenges us to consider is this: Why *shouldn't* we enjoy Christmas *even more* than children? Why shouldn't those with a firmer grasp of grace (if we have not grown too old for such things) not celebrate Christmas with *more* joy, *more* delight, *more* relish?

Consider Chesterton himself. Though he possessed one of the most brilliant minds of the twentieth century, he never lost his sense of childlike wonder. For all his brilliance, wit, and wisdom, he maintained a mischievous twinkle in his eyes. A spring in his step. He was unabashedly jolly. He personified mirth—for he saw the same lightness, the same sense of abiding joy, in God Himself. The sad reality is, most of us simply don't have time for the kind of joviality Chesterton embodied. We are too busy with the concerns of daily life to make space for merriment, room for levity. Our souls are too heavy for joy.

In C. S. Lewis's dedication of *The Lion, the Witch, and the Wardrobe* to his goddaughter Lucy, he muses that while she has grown too old for fairy tales, one day she might be old enough to start reading them again.[2] In Chesterton's poem "The Wise Men," he speaks of learned men who "peer and pore on tortured puzzles" and are well-versed in "labyrinthine lore," and "who know all things but the truth." After encountering the mind-boggling reality of the incarnation, these intellectual giants are reduced to "little children walking through the snow and rain."[3]

The paradox at the heart of Christlikeness is that the more one learns, the less one knows. The greatest saints are those who are the most childlike, and the most childlike are the most humble.

In an oft-quoted passage from *Orthodoxy*, Chesterton says,

Perhaps God is strong enough to exult in monotony. It is possible that God says every morning, "Do it again" to the sun; and every evening, "Do it again" to the moon. It may not be automatic necessity that makes all daisies alike; it may be that God makes every daisy separately, but has never got tired of making them. It may be that He has the eternal appetite of infancy; for we have sinned and grown old, and our Father is younger than we.[4]

Is it possible that we have matured past the capacity for wonder and surprise? Could it be that we have grown older than our Father? That we have lost our ability to behold, with childlike awe, the greatest fairy tale of all?

This Christmas season, give yourself permission to stop being sensible for a change and start being silly. Take a walk. Take a break. Smile, for heaven's sake. Find something to laugh about (preferably yourself). Recover the vitality of youth. Practice the "eternal appetite of infancy." Expand your capacity for wonder. Expand your capacity for pudding. Step outside and look at the stars. Follow one and see where it leads you. Go ice-skating on a frozen lake. Go sledding on a frozen backside. Drink hot chocolate with extra whipped cream and sprinkles. Roast marshmallows over an open fire. Sing a carol with gusto. Tell jokes (even bad ones). Shed some weight. Shed some worry. Get buoyant. After all, how else will you grow young enough to enter the kingdom of heaven? How else will you wholeheartedly embrace the joys of Christmas?

SCRIPTURE READING & REFLECTION

At that time the disciples came to Jesus, saying, "Who is the greatest in the kingdom of heaven?" And calling to him a child, he put him in the midst of them and said, "Truly, I say to you, unless you turn and become like children, you will never enter the kingdom of heaven. Whoever humbles himself like this child is the greatest in the kingdom of heaven."

MATTHEW 18:1-4

What do the children in your life enjoy about Christmas?

How might you foster a childlike faith in your life?

What are some ways you can wholeheartedly embrace the joys of Christmas this year?

✄ DAY 7 ✄

CONCERNING THE INESCAPABLE FRATERNITY OF THE FAMILY GATHERING

Christmas is utterly unsuited to the modern world. It presupposes the possibility of families being united, or reunited, and even of the men and women who chose each other being on speaking terms. Thus thousands of young adventurous spirits, ready to face the facts of human life, and encounter the vast variety of men and women as they really are, ready to fly to the ends of the earth and tolerate every alien or accidental quality in cannibals or devil-worshippers, are cruelly forced to face an hour, nay sometimes even two hours, in the society of Uncle George; or some aunt from Cheltenham whom they do not particularly like. Such abominable tortures cannot be tolerated in a time like ours. . . . It was never supposed that Parents were included in the great democratic abstraction called People. It was never supposed that brotherhood could extend to brothers.

G.K.'S WEEKLY (1933)[1]

The characters at the first Christmas were incongruous, to say the least. A young woman and her betrothed. Muddy shepherds from the hills. A smattering of animals. An assortment of angels. The nativity scene is striking (if not shocking) in its hodgepodge diversity. No one could foresee this gathering of unexpected guests, this fraternization of clean and unclean, sacred and profane. It serves as a prophetic picture of a church in which there would no longer be any Jew, Gentile, slave, free, male, female—but in which all would be one in Christ Jesus (Gal. 3:28).

Chesterton suggests that we, too, might find ourselves among unexpected (even unwelcome) guests at Christmas. We might rub elbows with a sworn enemy who, by a twist of fate, happens also to be a cousin. We might fall into tedious conversation with a ghastly personality we would, in any other circumstance, avoid at all costs— but who, at the moment, is quite unavoidable. Some of us would rather "fly to the ends of the earth and tolerate every alien or acci-dental quality in cannibals or devil-worshippers" than face an hour or two in the company of Uncle George or an intolerable aunt from Cheltenham. But that is precisely the point. At Christmas, we come to the same table, in the same spirit, to partake of the same meal. We must (at times against our will) recognize the common humanity of Uncle George or Aunty Intolerable—for as shocking as it may be, Christ came even for them. When God promised Abram that in him "all the families of the earth shall be blessed" (Gen. 12:3), the prom-ise extends even to the most insufferable examples of "all." What a sobering proposition, to tolerate the "abominable tortures" of rec-ognizing parents as part of "the great democratic abstraction called People," to extend the notion of "brotherhood even to brothers."

As Chesterton once noted, "The discordance or discomfort com-plained of by modern critics, in the family reunion, is not due to that mystical focal fire having been left burning, but to its having been left to go cold."[2] The unfortunate reality is that the "mystical focal fire" has not merely gone cold at Christmas, but in our culture at large. Families are broken, scattered, disconnected. If our gatherings are known for their discordance and discomfort, perhaps it is because many of us are living on the fading embers of a forsaken fire. In speaking of "heavy and heathen uncles" who would rather play golf than play make-believe with their nieces and nephews, Chesterton muses:

> Let them play golf day after day; let them play golf for three
> hundred and sixty-four days, and nights as well, with balls
> dipped in luminous paint, to be pursued in the dark. But
> let there be one night when things grow luminous from
> within: and one day when men seek for all that is buried
> in themselves; and discover, where she is indeed hidden,
> behind locked gates and shuttered windows, and doors
> thrice barred and bolted, the spirit of liberty.[3]

In a world of increasing disconnectedness, the very act of gathering together at Christmas is an act of defiance. Christmas is an opportunity to lay our grudges aside—to open our arms, minds, and hearts to those we are yoked to, however incongruously. Whatever your gathering looks like this year, extend grace to those around you. Listen to a long, rambling story when you'd rather plug your ears. Take a seat next to Uncle George. Make a plate for Aunty Intolerable. Seek out discomfort like you have a sixth sense for it. Allow "things to grow luminous from within" and perhaps you might discover "the spirit of liberty" at work "behind locked gates and shuttered windows."

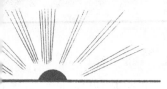

SCRIPTURE READING & REFLECTION

Let us consider how to stir one another to love and good works, not neglecting to meet together, as is the habit of some, but encouraging one another, and all the more as you see the Day drawing near.

HEBREWS 10:24-25

Consider some ways you might open your arms, mind, and heart to family during this season.

Make a mental list of the most intolerable of your family members. What would it take for you to lay aside your own comfort and extend grace to them at Christmas?

How might you make the most of your time "behind locked gates and shuttered windows"?

AS FOR GAMES AND THE POSSIBLE INVENTION OF NEW ONES

It is not so much old things as new things that a real Christmas might create. It might, for instance, create new games, if people were really driven to invent their own games. Most of the very old games began with the use of ordinary tools or furniture. So the very terms of tennis were founded on the framework of the old inn courtyard. So, it is said, the stumps in cricket were originally only the three legs of the milking-stool. Now we might invent new things of this kind, if we remembered who is the mother of invention. How pleasing it would be to start a game in which we scored so much for hitting the umbrella-stand or the dinner-wagon, or even the host and hostess; of course, with a missile of some soft material. Children who are lucky enough to be left alone in the nursery invent not only whole games, but whole dramas and life-stories of their own; they invent secret languages; they create imaginary families; they laboriously conduct family magazines. That is the sort of creative spirit that we want in the modern world; want both in the sense of desiring and in the sense of lacking it. If Christmas could become more domestic, instead of less, I believe there would be a vast increase in the real Christmas spirit; the spirit of the Child.

THE THING (1929)[1]

We have the Victorian age to thank for many of our Christmas traditions, such as Christmas cards, the decorated Christmas tree, and of course, Charles Dickens's *A Christmas Carol*—but the parlor games of the Victorian era have largely been forgotten: games such as Squeak, Piggy, Squeak, in which blindfolded players would guess at the identity of the individual squealing like a pig, or Snapdragon, a particularly dangerous affair in which players would bravely reach into a flaming bowl of brandy to retrieve a raisin, or Up Jenkins, in which one team would furtively pass a coin under the table while the other team guessed who was in possession of it.[2] Chesterton describes "solid and solemn city men . . . required to take part in the game of Honey-Pots, which involves sitting on the floor, hunched up in a squatting attitude at the risk of being rolled over, as if the fairies had indeed turned them into pots of honey, instead of leaving them with the dismal distinction of having pots of money. Some great millionaire, equipped with the brain of steel and the will of iron which are part of the apparatus of his profession, might none the less be required to play one of the old nursery games. He might be condemned to playing Puss-in-the-Corner instead of playing Plutocrat-in-the-Corner; in whatever Wheat-Corner or Milk-Corner he might be at the moment benefiting mankind."[3]

He reminds us that many of these games involved household objects, and that even more popular games such as tennis began in the courtyard of an old inn, that cricket stumps began as the legs of a milking stool.

The point is, these games emerged from necessity (which Chesterton reminds us is the mother of invention)—and that is precisely what could happen again if Christmas "could become more domestic." With families gathered behind closed doors, perhaps there would be a "vast increase in Christmas spirit." Like children trapped in a nursery, perhaps we might be left alone long enough to concoct not just new games, but even new dramas and new languages. As Chesterton once expressed, "I have never understood what people mean by domesticity being tame; it seems to me one of the wildest of adventures."[4] This is why he says that a real Christmas has the potential to create not old things but new things, for Christmas is inextricably linked to "the spirit of the child." "If you had the antiquarian curiosity to ask why there was this tradition of people being childish," he once wrote, "you would trace it back to a tremendous, a mysterious and even a paradoxical doctrine; that on this strange night even God became a Child."[5]

Writing elsewhere, he reminds us that it was largely poor households that gave us these time-honored traditions:

> It is to long pedigrees of peasants that we owe the survival of nearly all the jokes and games that occupy children (and the wiser adults) in any middle-class house at Christmas. It is a mere fact of English history that the idea of a Merry Christmas was maintained much more faithfully by the ragged carol-singers than it was by the Merry Gentlemen to whom they sang their carols.[6]

The truth of the matter is, "The only real fun is to have limited materials and a good idea. . . . What is really funny about Christmas charades in any average home is that there is a contrast between commonplace resources and one comic idea. What is deadly dull about the millionaire-banquets is that there is a contrast between colossal resources and no idea."[7]

By all means, let us close our doors at Christmas, but let us fling wide our imaginations. May we be so bold as to not only honor old traditions, but invent new ones. May every staircase be a mountain slope, every ball of yarn a cannonball, every candy cane a harpoon, every aunt a pirate, every uncle a dragon, for "on this strange night even God became a Child."[8]

SCRIPTURE READING & REFLECTION

And in the same region there were shepherds out in the field, keeping watch over their flock by night. And an angel of the Lord appeared to them, and the glory of the Lord shone around them, and they were filled with great fear. And the angel said to them, "Fear not, for behold, I bring you good news of great joy that will be for all the people. For unto you is born this day in the city of David a Savior, who is Christ the Lord. And this will be a sign for you: you will find a baby wrapped in swaddling cloths and lying in a manger." And suddenly there was with the angel a multitude of the heavenly host praising God and saying,

"Glory to God in the highest,
and on earth peace among those with whom he is pleased!"

LUKE 2:8-14

Consider the significance that the first words the angel says to the shepherds are "fear not." How would you have reacted?

How might you lay aside a spirit of fear and foster "the spirit of a child" not just at Christmas but also throughout the year?

What are some traditions or games you could incorporate into your holiday season?

⚔ DAY 9 ⚔

ON CHRISTMAS AS
A DECLARATION OF WAR

All this indescribable thing that we call the Christmas
atmosphere only hangs in the air as something like a lingering
fragrance or fading vapor from the exultant explosion of
that one hour in the Judean hills nearly two thousand years
ago. But the savor is still unmistakable, and it is something
too subtle or too solitary to be covered by our use of the
word peace. By the very nature of the story the rejoicings in
the cavern were rejoicings in a fortress or an outlaw's den;
properly understood it is not unduly flippant to say they
were rejoicings in a dug-out. It is not only true that such a
subterranean chamber was a hiding-place from enemies; and
that the enemies were already scouring the stony plain that
lay above it like a sky. It is not only that the very horse-hoofs
of Herod might in that sense have passed like thunder over the
sunken head of Christ. It is also that there is in that image a
true idea of an outpost, of a piercing through the rock and an
entrance into an enemy territory. There is in this buried divinity an idea of undermining the world; of shaking the towers

47

and palaces from below; even as Herod the great king felt that earthquake under him and swayed with his swaying palace.

THE EVERLASTING MAN (1925)[1]

If the carol "Silent Night" is any indication, the first Christmas was calm, bright, tender, mild, peaceful. We've seen countless depictions of the seraphic baby Jesus, enveloped in a halo of light, or the joyous choir of angels above, swathed in luminescent robes. So entrenched in us are these serene pictures of Christmas that it is tempting to believe the story is merely one of "peace on earth and goodwill to men." Chesterton reminds us that evil lurks in the background of our familiar nativity scenes; that just beyond the spill of holy light, an enemy who has "rotted the legends with lust and frozen the theories into atheism"[2] conspires with all the forces of hell to wage his counterattack.

We are comfortable with the "humility, gaiety, and gratitude" of Christmas—but a Christmas of "mystical fear, vigilance, and drama"? A Christmas in which Satan himself steals onto the stage? That's beyond imaginable for most of us—but that is precisely what Chesterton encourages us to envision. The cave where Christ was born was not merely a sanctuary, but a fortress. He was, quite literally, born in "enemy territory," his birth nothing short of an "exultant explosion." In the words of C. S. Lewis, "Christianity is the story of how the rightful king has landed, you might say landed in disguise, and is calling us all to take part in a great campaign of sabotage."[3] The story of Christmas is not a cozy fairy tale but an exhilarating romance about a king who came to claim His rightful throne and rescue His beloved.

If we miss this aspect of Christmas, we risk "missing the point of Christmas" altogether. It is not just that Christ came into the world to offer salvation, to atone for our sins, to welcome us into the family of God; He came to vanquish evil, scatter darkness, defeat death. When He drew His first breath, the depths of hell trembled. He who was born in that "subterranean chamber," that "outlaw's den," came on a mission to "undermine the world" and all that is of the world. "Towers and palaces shook from below." "Herod the great king felt that earthquake under him and swayed with his swaying palace." Christmas was a declaration of war.

The enemy's counterstrike came swiftly and mercilessly: Herod, fearful that his reign would be challenged by the prophesied Messiah and deceived by the wise men as to the whereabouts of the infant king, went on a killing spree, commanding his men to murder all male children aged two years and under in Bethlehem. That he operated under the influence of hell is hardly a matter for debate (as Chesterton says, "The demons, in that first festival of Christmas, feasted also in their own fashion"[4]). The gospel of Matthew recounts this "massacre of the innocents," which was foretold by the prophet Jeremiah:

> "A voice was heard in Ramah,
> weeping and loud lamentation,
> Rachel weeping for her children;
> she refused to be comforted, because they are no more."
> (Matt. 2:18)

It serves as a sobering reminder that Christ was born into a vio-lent, godless world—a world in which kings clung to power with clenched fist, in which the weak and vulnerable were trampled, in which wickedness held sway over the earth. At a surface glance, not much has changed since then. Our world is just as broken, our leaders just as corrupt, our soil just as blood-soaked. Every day, the innocent are trampled. Every day, a new Rachel weeps for her chil-dren. But Christmas reminds us this is not the end of the story—that there will be a day when suffering ends, when evil is leached from every vein of creation, when the children of the King (in the words of George MacDonald) "creep from our chrysalis, and spread the great heaven-storming wings of the psyches of God."[5]

In light of this great hope, we can proclaim that there will, indeed, be "peace on earth and goodwill to men"—but it will be won not by a meek and mild Jesus, but by the triumphant King of kings and Lord of lords, whose kingdom will have no end.

SCRIPTURE READING & REFLECTION

For to us a child is born,
to us a son is given;
and the government shall be upon his shoulder,
and his name shall be called
Wonderful Counselor, Mighty God,
Everlasting Father, Prince of Peace.
Of the increase of his government and of peace
there will be no end,
on the throne of David and over his kingdom,
to establish it and to uphold it
with justice and with righteousness
from this time forth and forevermore.
The zeal of the LORD of hosts will do this.

ISAIAH 9:6-7

Consider the implications of the phrase "the government shall be upon his shoulder." What impact does this prophecy have on the nations of the world?

Meditate on what the threat of the "exultant explosion" of the incarnation poses to the powers of darkness holding sway over the earth.

How might you view Christmas as something not meek and mild, but full of "mystical fear, vigilance, and drama"?

◇◈ DAY 10 ◈◇

ON CHRISTMAS AS
AN ANTIDOTE TO A
DISENCHANTED IMAGINATION

Children still understand the feast of Christmas, they still
sometimes feast to excess in the matter of plum pudding or
a turkey. But there is never anything in the least frivolous
about their attitude to a plum pudding or a turkey. Still less
is there anything frivolous in their attitude to a stocking or
a Christmas tree. They have the serious and even solemn
sense of the great truth; that Christmas is a time when things
happen; things that do not always happen.

G.K.'S WEEKLY (1925)[1]

In his seminal work *A Secular Age*, philosopher Charles Taylor
observes that one of the defining characteristics of the premodern
world was its *enchanted-ness*.[2] Before the rising tide of secularism
spread its shadow across Western culture, the self (and the world)
was largely seen as *porous*.[3] The universe was not a closed system,
but a place where the veil between the natural and the supernatural

51

was thin at best, where spirits (good or evil) could come and go as they pleased. That world was perhaps overzealous in regard to superstition or uninformed in regard to science, but the fact of the matter is, it was a place where religious belief was not only plausible, but taken for granted.[4]

By contrast, the *disenchanted posture* of modernity fancies that science and reason can provide an easy answer to virtually every question, that all that exists can be deduced to what can be empirically known by the mind of man. In the "social imaginary" of the modern world,[5] in which humanity is continually progressing toward a brighter tomorrow, we have banished all angels and demons, exiled all gods; we have covered over the thin places and deprived the world of mystery. As Chesterton says in *What's Wrong with the World*, "The future is a refuge from the fierce competition of our forefathers . . . I can make the future as narrow as myself; the past is obliged to be as broad and turbulent as humanity."[6]

In relation to Christmas, he speaks of children having a serious and solemn understanding of the season, because it "is a time when things happen; things that do not always happen." Christmas is not an abstract observance of something-or-other, but a conscious commemoration of something-in-particular: a specific event that happened at a specific time in the course of human history; an event that defies logic and resists all naturalistic explanations: God so loved the world that He sent His Son to us, who was conceived by the Holy Spirit in the womb of a virgin, was born on a particular night, at a particular time, in a particular place.

As Chesterton says elsewhere, "These two words (Christmas Day) express better than any religious periphrasis the peculiar richness and intensity which clings round the story of Bethlehem. . . . Above all, it expresses that quality of instantaneousness, of urgency and excitement, which distinguishes Christmas from so many of the earth's festivals: the sentiment that it does not celebrate some event a thousand years back, but some event that has just happened, some event that happens every year."[7] Such a thing could only happen in an enchanted world—a world where such things do not *always* happen, and yet a world where miracles *do*, in fact, occur—even if they are, by definition, the exception to the rule.

Today, many people who claim to believe in God are functional deists, envisioning the world as an intricate machine of sorts—designed and established by God, but left to its own devices. Christmas begs to differ. Christmas proclaims that God is not distant or removed, but intimately involved in His creation. Christmas is a proclamation that we do not live in a closed universe, but a universe upheld "by the word of his power" (Heb. 1:3). As Chesterton expresses in *Orthodoxy*, "I felt in my bones . . . that this world does not explain itself. It may be a miracle with a supernatural explanation; it may be a conjuring trick, with a natural explanation. But the explanation of the conjuring trick, if it is to satisfy me, will have to be better than the natural explanations I have heard. The thing is magic, true or false."[8]

Chesterton suggests that in the end, the purely naturalistic accounts simply do not do justice to the utter miracle of the world, the staggering beauty of creation, the astonishing gift of consciousness. He goes on to say,

> I had always vaguely felt facts to be miracles in the sense
> that they are wonderful: now I began to think them
> miracles in the stricter sense that they were willful. . . . In
> short, I had always believed that the world involved magic:
> now I thought that perhaps it involved a magician. . . . I
> had always felt life first as a story: and if there is a story
> there is a story-teller.[9]

Christmas is a reminder that the cosmos we inhabit is not a disenchanted place, but a magical realm governed by a real Magician, a narrative tapestry conceived by a master Storyteller. Today, let us join Chesterton in embracing Christmas with the serious, solemn, enchanted wonder of a child.

SCRIPTURE READING & REFLECTION

Now the birth of Jesus Christ took place in this way. When his mother Mary had been betrothed to Joseph, before they came together she was found to be with child from the Holy Spirit. And her husband Joseph, being a just man and unwilling to put her to shame, resolved to divorce her quietly. But as he considered these things, behold, an angel of the Lord appeared to him in a dream, saying, "Joseph, son of David, do not fear to take Mary as your wife, for that which is conceived in her is from the Holy Spirit. She will bear a son, and you shall call his name Jesus, for he will save his people from their sins."

MATTHEW 1:18-21

Take a moment and consider the staggering claims of this story: that Christ, the eternal Word, one with the Father, was born as a human being (from the womb of a virgin) and came to save us from our sins.

What would your life look like if you truly treated the universe as an enchanted place?

How might you grow in your faith if you viewed God not as distant, but intimately involved in His creation (and in your life)?

~⊰ DAY 11 ⊱~

A BRIEF CELEBRATION
OF THE BOOMERANG

The return of old things in new times, by an established and
automatic machinery, is the permanent security of men who
like to be sane. The greatest of all blessings is the boomerang.
And all the healthiest things we know are boomerangs—that
is, they are things that return. Sleep is a boomerang. We fling
it from us at morning, and it knocks us down again at night.
Daylight is a boomerang. We see it at the end of the day dis-
appearing in the distance; and at the beginning of the next day
we see it come back and break the sky. I mean, we see it if we
get up early enough—which I have done once or twice. The
same sort of sensational sanity (truly to be called sensational
because it braces and strengthens all the sensations) is given
by the return of religious and social festivals. To have such an
institution as Christmas is, I will not say to make an accident
inevitable, but I will say to make an adventure recurrent—
and therefore, in one sense, to make an adventure everlasting.

THE ILLUSTRATED LONDON NEWS (1913)[1]

After the Israelites were delivered from the hand of Pharaoh, the Lord God commanded them to keep the Passover as a reminder of their miraculous liberation from bondage. In time, the Hebrew calendar would be populated with various feasts and festivals celebrating the faithfulness of God. These rituals were, in Chesterton's words, *boomerangs:* "things that return." Our church calendar is likewise marked by numerous seasons and rituals of remembrance. By structuring our days and weeks and years in such a way, we are declaring that time itself is governed by God. As the Israelites' festivals were a perpetual retelling of the same story, so are our Christian traditions a form of continually re-grounding ourselves in the narrative of redemption. The consistent "return of old things in new times," Chesterton tells us, "is the permanent security of men who like to be sane." Like the cyclical return of daylight and sleep (even for a late riser like Chesterton), the regularity of our holiday rituals is a way of maintaining godly sanity in an unstable and unpredictable world. While modernity is infatuated with the fads and fashions of our cultural moment, may we be ever more committed to that which is old and unfashionable—for in these time-honored traditions, these "ancient paths" (Jer. 6:16), is found a "sensational sanity."

Christmas is just such a path. As Chesterton expresses in *Heretics,*

> In the round of our rational and mournful year one festival remains out of all those ancient gaieties that once covered the whole earth. Christmas remains to remind us of those ages, whether pagan or Christian, when the many acted poetry instead of the few writing it. In all the winter in our woods there is no tree in glow but the holly.[2]

If you have ever felt a pang of longing at the thought of the coming Christmas season, if you have eagerly awaited it with the restlessness of a child, then you have participated in the blessed longing of Advent. If you have woken on Christmas morning with a flutter of expectation for what the day ahead holds, you have partaken in the wondrous experience of the abiding and ancient institution of Christmas. Chesterton calls such institutions "recurrent, everlasting adventures," an apt expression of the gospel itself. The invitation extended to us through the death and resurrection of Christ is to embark on the everlasting adventure of union with God, to journey deeper into the "mystery hidden for ages and now revealed to his saints" (Col. 1:26). The incarnation is but the opening scene in that drama, the first taste of the stirring saga to come. In God's kingdom, we are invited not just to "write poetry," but to "act" it—not just to be spectators in the story He is telling, but to play a vital role in it.

So, let us raise a toast in celebration of the sacred boomerangs that are our Christmas traditions. While the world busies itself with passing things, may we tread and retread the ancient paths of the faith. May we remember *what* we remember. May we remember *why* we remember. May remembrance *re-member* us. May we join with all the saints in the recurrent, everlasting adventure of Christmas.

SCRIPTURE READING & REFLECTION

"These words that I command you today shall be on your heart. You shall teach them diligently to your children, and shall talk of them when you sit in your house, and when you walk by the way, and when you lie down, and when you rise. You shall bind them as a sign on your hand, and they shall be as frontlets between your eyes. You shall write them on the doorposts of your house and on your gates."

DEUTERONOMY 6:6-9

The Israelites were instructed to keep the words of God near them at all times. What are some daily reminders of God's Word that you could incorporate into your Christmas season?

How can you make Christmas an "everlasting adventure" for your loved ones this year?

Consider Chesterton's statement that festivals such as Christmas are "the permanent security of men who like to be sane." How might Christmas help you maintain godly sanity?

IN REGARD TO
THE ENORMOUS
AND OVERWHELMING
EVERYTHING

Even those who can only regard the great story of Bethlehem as a fairy-tale told by the fire will yet agree that such narrowness is the first artistic necessity even of a good fairy-tale. But there are others who think, at least, that their thought strikes deeper and pierces to a more subtle truth in the mind. There are others for whom all our fairy-tales, and even all our appetite for fairy-tales, draw their fire from one central fairy-tale, as all forgeries draw their significance from a signature. They believe that this fable is a fact, and that the other fables cannot really be appreciated even as fables until we know it is a fact. For them, personality is a step beyond universality; one might almost call it an escape from universality. And what they follow is as much something more than Pantheism as a flame is something more than a temperature. For them, God is not bound down and limited by being merely everything; He is also at liberty to be something.

> And for them Christmas will always deal with a reality exactly
> as Shakespeare's poetry deals with an unreality; it will give,
> not to airy nothing, but to the enormous and overwhelming
> everything, a local habitation and a Name.

THE USES OF DIVERSITY (1920)[1]

For as long as human beings have roamed the earth, we have been telling stories: stories scrawled on cave walls, whispered over communal fires, penned with quill and ink, painted, acted, sung. The story-shaped psychology of humankind is more than mere coincidence. As Chesterton says in *The Everlasting Man*, "A monkey does not draw clumsily and a man cleverly; a monkey does not begin the art of representation and a man carry it to perfection. A monkey does not do it at all; he does not begin to do it at all; he does not begin to begin to do it at all . . . art is the signature of man."[2]

The birth of Christ is a story of notable specificity—but then, as Chesterton reminds us, such a thing "is the first artistic necessity" of any "good fairy-tale." As he muses elsewhere, "Modern theology will tell us the Child of Bethlehem is only an abstraction of all children; that the mother from Nazareth is a metaphysical symbol of motherhood. The truth is that it is only because the Nativity is a narrative of one lonely and literal mother and child that it is universal to all. If Bethlehem were not particular it would not be popular."[3] So, there is a particularity to the Christmas story. Its popularity is, perhaps, partly due to its particularity—but that hardly means the story is true, in the way that "the sky is blue" or "2+2=4" are true. We must ask: Why is the Christ story any different from the mass of fairy tales, myths, and legends from antiquity? In a secular, materialist view of reality, these stories are seen as the feeble attempts of finite human beings to reckon with the terrifying futility of existence, to impose some semblance of meaning on an ultimately meaningless universe.

But Chesterton speaks of those for whom the Christ story "strikes a deeper" chord, for whom it "pierces to a more subtle truth in the mind," for whom it is not simply another fairy tale or legend, but the one archetypical story from which all stories "draw their fire, as all forgeries draw their significance from a signature." In this view, the religious stories that developed throughout human history are dim reflections of a true story they were anticipating, unaware. As C. S. Lewis articulated, "If my religion is erroneous then occurrences of similar motifs in pagan stories are, of course, instances of the same, or a similar error. But if my religion is true, then these stories may well be a *preparatio evangelica*, a divine hinting in poetic and ritual form at the same central truth which was later focused and (so to speak) historicized in the Incarnation."[4]

Chesterton writes, "I say you cannot really understand any myths till you have found that one of them is not a myth. Turnip ghosts[5] mean nothing if there are no real ghosts. Forged bank-notes mean nothing if there are no real bank-notes. Heathen gods mean nothing, and must always mean nothing, to those of us that deny the Christian God. When once a god is admitted, even a false god, the Cosmos begins to know its place: which is the second place. When once it is the real God the Cosmos falls down before Him, offering flowers in spring as flames in winter."[6] As he says elsewhere, "our souls do not come from everywhere, but from somewhere . . . the method of our salvation was truly local and personal, and not cosmic and impersonal."[7]

If we are made by a Creator God, then it should come as no surprise that we are "sub-creators," to use Tolkien's term. In his words, "Fantasy remains a human right: we make in our measure and in our derivative mode, because we are made: and not only made, but made in the image and likeness of a Maker."[8] The Maker of heaven and earth is not an abstract presence, but a startling, singular personality—a Name above all names: ruler of the "enormous and overwhelming everything."

Today, let us meditate on the "one central fairy-tale," which is a fact, the story from which all others "draw their fire"—and let us marvel that we, story-shaped sub-creators, so image our Father in heaven. Pull up a chair and get comfortable. It's a good story.

SCRIPTURE READING & REFLECTION

So Paul, standing in the midst of the Areopagus, said: "Men of Athens, I perceive that in every way you are very religious. For as I passed along and observed the objects of your worship, I found also an altar with this inscription: 'To the unknown god.' What therefore you worship as unknown, this I proclaim to you. The God who made the world and everything in it, being Lord of heaven and earth, does not live in temples made by man, nor is he served by human hands, as though he needed anything, since he himself gives to all mankind life and breath and everything. And he made from one man every nation of mankind to live on all the face of the earth, having determined allotted periods and the boundaries of their dwelling place, that they should seek God, and perhaps feel their way toward him and find him."

ACTS 17:22-27

Take a moment and reflect on the idea of God as creator and story-teller. What are some of your favorite stories that point to Christ?

What are some ways that you image God on a daily basis through "sub-creation"? How might you better use those gifts for His glory?

Paul told the men of Athens that God intends for human beings to seek Him and find Him—not unlike the shepherds and the wise men who came to worship the infant Christ. Consider how Christmas is an invitation to discover the one true God and become part of His story.

ON THE JUXTAPOSITION OF FRIGHTFUL WEATHER AND FESTIVE GAIETY

The cards that spangle Bethlehem with frost are generally regarded by the learned merely as vulgar lies. . . . But even in the cruder and more concrete sense the tradition about the December snow is not quite so false as is suggested. It is not a mere local illusion for Englishmen to picture the Holy Child in a snowstorm, as it would be for the Londoners to picture him in a London fog. There can be snow in Jerusalem, and there might be snow in Bethlehem; and when we penetrate to the idea behind the image, we find it is not only possible but probable. In Palestine, at least in these mountainous parts of Palestine, men have the same general sentiment about the seasons as in the West or the North. Snow is a rarity, but winter is a reality. Whether we regard it as the divine purpose of a mystery or the human purpose of a myth, the purpose of putting such a feast in winter would be just the same in Bethlehem as it would be in Balham. Any one thinking of the Holy Child as born in December would mean by it exactly

what we mean by it; that Christ is not merely a summer sun
of the prosperous but a winter fire for the unfortunate.

THE NEW JERUSALEM (1920)[1]

I n literature, winter is often associated with death, darkness, and
hopelessness. In William Wordsworth's poem "Lucy Grey", a child
embarks in a blizzard with merely a lantern to light her way, only to
be lost in the swirling snows:

The storm came on before its time:
She wandered up and down;
And many a hill did Lucy climb:
But never reached the town.[2]

James Joyce's short story "The Dead" concludes with the chilling
line, "His soul swooned slowly as he heard the snow falling faintly
through the universe and faintly falling, like the descent of their last
end, upon all the living and the dead."[3] Hans Christian Anderson's
"The Snow Queen" involves a wicked enchantress who travels with
the snows of winter and dwells in a palace of ice—a clear influence
on the White Witch in C. S. Lewis's Narnia series. In *The Lion,
the Witch, and the Wardrobe*, the faun Tumnus laments that under
the White Witch's rule it is "always winter and never Christmas."[4]
Winter, in its harshest form, is cold and merciless, freezing the life
out of the world. In the words of Victor Hugo, "winter changes into
stone the water of heaven and the heart of man."[5]

Spring, on the other hand, is a time of vitality and rebirth, as
beautifully illustrated by the stirring turn of events in Lewis's novel,
as the Witch's control over Narnia begins to wane and the snow
begins to melt, little by little, until the land is green again (the chapter in which this occurs is titled "The Spell Begins to Break"). In the
words of poet Gerard Manley Hopkins:

Nothing is so beautiful as Spring—
When weeds, in wheels, shoot long and lovely and lush.[6]

In the Song of Solomon, the lover calls his beloved away with the proclamation that "the winter is past" and now "the flowers appear on the earth, the time of singing has come" (Song 2:10–13). That winter has come to be associated in our minds with feelings of warmth and cheer is largely the result of Christmas. We do not think fondly of ice and snow and frosted windows because we have a particular fondness for the cold, but because we are shielded from it by roaring fires and cups of hot cocoa and friendly conversation. As Chesterton once said, "it is based upon a contrast, a contrast between the fire and wine within the house and the winter and the roaring rains without. It is far more poetical, because there is in it a note of defense, almost of war; a note of being besieged by the snow and hail; of making merry in the belly of a fort."[7] This juxtaposition of ideas—of bitter cold and cloistered comfort—is one of the hall-marks of the Christmas season. Christmas, indeed, is a "winter fire."

We must remember that Christ arrived at a harrowing time in human history, for the Jews in particular. Their land was under Roman rule. Many of their religious leaders had become complacent at best and cor-rupt at worst. Their prophecies of a miraculous deliverer had not come to pass (some questioned if they ever would). It was a time of desola-tion. Of cold hearts. Withered faith. It was, in more ways than one, "the winter of their discontent." Into this bleak and desperate world Christ appeared and lit a fire that has not gone out these two thousand years. The power of the imagery holds, whether we believe He was, in fact, born in December or that snow in Bethlehem is a "vulgar lie." The winter fire of Christmas reminds us that while frost may blanket the once fruitful land, that the streams may be frozen solid and every tree stripped to the bone, the long winter will one day come to an end. Flowers will appear again. The time of singing will come.

Today, as snow lies heavy on the earth (literally or figuratively), light a candle in observance of Christmas. Remember Christ, the light of the world, who "is not merely a summer sun of the prosperous but a winter fire for the unfortunate." After all, as Chesterton says, "The best way to shorten winter is to prolong Christmas."[8]

SCRIPTURE READING & REFLECTION

"Arise, my love, my beautiful one,
and come away,
for behold, the winter is past;
the rain is over and gone.
The flowers appear on the earth,
the time of singing has come . . ."

SONG OF SOLOMON 2:10-13

Have you struggled with a "winter of discontent" in your life? How was Christ a "winter fire" to come home to during that season?

How can you help a friend or neighbor through the long winter?

Consider the promise that the winter of sin and death and darkness will one day come to an end and the kingdom of heaven will be established in the earth. How does this affect your view of Christmas?

66

ᒡᔈ DAY 14 ᐚᔈ

CONCERNING HEARTY BREAKFASTS AND THE PLEASURES OF BEING FLUNG HEADLONG INTO THE SEA

If there are two godlike and glorious things in the world they are an English breakfast and a sea-bath. Yet I have never known any brave and honourable man who denied that he detested getting out of bed and plunging into cold water. The forms and rites of Christmas Day are meant merely to give the last push to people who are afraid to be festive. Father Christmas exists to haul us out of bed and make us partake of meals too beautiful to be called breakfasts. He exists to fling us out of the bathing-machine into the heady happiness of the sea.

THE ILLUSTRATED LONDON NEWS (1910)[1]

Human beings are creatures of habit. Our days are filled with observed traditions, evidenced in everything from the preparation of coffee to the preparation of rest. We are quasireligious in our regularity, borderline liturgical in our observance of the ritualistic rhythms and practiced patterns of our everyday lives. Chesterton calls an English breakfast and a sea-bath two of the most "godlike and glorious things in the world" (a proper English breakfast consists of beans, toast, mushrooms, tomatoes, potatoes, bacon, eggs, and black pudding. A sea-bath, I assume, needs no explanation). But it should go without saying that in each case, a step must be taken prior to enjoyment: in order to eat, one must wake; in order to bathe in the sea, one must plunge into cold water. The initiative may be made easier by habit, but it is not involuntary. One can choose to remain in bed all day. One can choose to remain hungry. We are creatures of habit, and habits can be broken.

But such is not the case with Christmas. Christmas arrives whether we welcome it or not, whether we are prepared for it or not, whether we are ready, in spirit and in soul, to embrace it or not. If we are unready, Christmas refuses to be moved to a more convenient date on the calendar. If we are not in the right state of mind, Christmas will not wait around for us to summon the adequate cheer with which to greet it. Christmas is notoriously inconsiderate in this regard. And for this, we should be eternally grateful—for try as we might, joy does not always come naturally to us. We are not always in the mood for revelry. Our natural disposition is rarely the personification of cheerfulness. On this point it is crucial to remember that habits only become habits through repetition. The more we practice joy, the more effortlessly it will come to us. The more we revel, the more we will become revelers. The more we embody cheerfulness, the more naturally we will be of good cheer. Thank God that Christmas descends so inconsiderately upon us, giving a "last push" to those "afraid to be festive"—for often we are numbered among them.

The abruptness of Christmas, its merry insensitivity, is part of its power. As Chesterton once remarked, "It is the very essence of a festival that it breaks upon one brilliantly and abruptly, that at one moment the great day is not and the next moment the great day is."[2]

Christmas comes but once a year, but it comes every year, and that is precisely the point. "The thing is done at a particular time so that people may be conscious of a particular truth; as is the case with all ceremonial observances, such as the Silence of Armistice Day or the signal of a salute with the guns or the sudden noise of bells for the New Year. They are all meant to fix the mind upon the fact of the feast or memorial, and suggest that a passing moment has a meaning when it would otherwise be meaningless."[3]

All of this applies to those of us who celebrate Christmas reverently (if imperfectly). "Let us be consistent, therefore, about Christmas, and either keep customs or not keep them," Chesterton once wrote. "If you do not like sentiment and symbolism, you do not like Christmas; go away and celebrate something else."[4] If we are determined to take Christmas seriously, we have no choice but to be "sufficiently ritualistic," regardless of our current mental and emotional state. We may stay in bed, but it will not stop Christmas from coming. We can bury our heads in the pillows, but it will not stop the feast from being served. If we know what's good for us, we will let Father Christmas "haul us out of bed," stuff us with "meals too beautiful to be called breakfasts" and "fling us into the heady happiness of the sea."

SCRIPTURE READING & REFLECTION

Do not neglect the gift you have, which was given you by prophecy when the council of elders laid their hands on you. Practice these things, immerse yourself in them, so that all may see your progress. Keep a close watch on yourself and on the teaching. Persist in this, for by so doing you will save both yourself and your hearers.

1 TIMOTHY 4:14–16

Consider how you might "practice joy" this Christmas season.

What are some areas of your walk with God where you have grown through simple obedience?

Knowing that Christmas will "arrive abruptly," how might you prepare your heart to receive it?

A WORD ON
THE WORD MADE FLESH

There was no purely human tradition of any purely human
Jesus. In so far as there was any tradition at all, lingering
in the fights and factions of Greek and Judaic religion, it
was the tradition of a purely divine Jesus. It was a tradition
furiously upheld by all those traditionalists who wished
to represent Him as wholly and solely divine. Only the
orthodoxy of the Catholic and Apostolic Church declared
that He was in the least human. And above all, for this is the
point of the paradox, the Catholic Church proclaimed that
original humanity more and more loudly, as it passed away
from its original human habitation. As the Church marched
westward she bore with her, with ever-increasing exultation
and certitude, the human corporeal thing that had been made
flesh in Bethlehem; and left behind a ghost for the Gnostics
and a god like a gilded idol for the Greek heretics, and for the
Moslems only the fading shadow of a prophet.

CHRISTENDOM IN DUBLIN (1932)[1]

Throughout the history of the church, many of the greatest heresies have been those related to the divinity of Christ. Some emphasized His divinity at the expense of His humanity. Some His humanity at the expense of His divinity. But never was there a heresy that claimed Jesus was purely human. A theological doctrine of a purely human Jesus is a contradiction in terms. This is what Chesterton means when he says that "there was no purely human tradition of any purely human Jesus." Such a tradition would not need to be codified into doctrine, any more than the fact of my existence needs to be codified into doctrine. The great mystery at the heart of the incarnation is that Christ was both fully human *and* fully divine: two natures intertwined, indivisible, inseparable. This paradoxical reality is a doctrine known as the hypostatic union, which comes from the Greek *hypóstasis*, meaning "substance, foundation, substructure."[2] It's the word used by the author of Hebrews to describe Christ as being "the radiance of the glory of God and the exact imprint of his nature [*hypóstasis*]" (Heb. 1:3).

If there has been a temptation to heresy, it has been to treat Jesus not as fully human, but as wholly divine. There is a certain embarrassment about the idea that God would take on human flesh, with all its fragility and dependency, that the Creator of all things would subject Himself to the need for oxygen and food and sleep and sunlight—but that is the staggering truth at the heart of the Christmas story: that God, in all His glory, stooped to the level of becoming a "human corporeal thing made in flesh in Bethlehem." That the child born of Mary—a child of flesh and blood and cell and sinew—was, by some profound, impenetrable mystery, "the radiance of the glory of God and the exact imprint of his nature." He who is the life and breath of all living things became a living, breathing thing. He who knits together the child in the womb was Himself knit together, in fearful and wonderful glory (Ps. 139:13–14). In Chesterton's words, "we can never reach the end even of our own ideas about the child who was a father and the mother who was a child."[3]

Christmas reminds us that our God is not a "ghost" or "a gilded idol" or "the fading shadow of a prophet." He is not merely human—for then He would be unworthy of our worship. He is not merely divine—for then He would be a stranger to our weakness. The child born in Bethlehem was the eternal Word, one with the Father, who took on flesh and dwelt among us—"that he might become a merciful and faithful high priest" (Heb. 2:17), "to redeem those who were under the law, so that we might receive adoption" as children of God (Gal. 4:5).

As Chesterton so eloquently expresses in *The New Jerusalem*,

> What has survived through an age of atheism as the most indestructible would survive through an age of polytheism as the most indispensable. If among many gods it could not presently be proved to be the strongest, some would still know it was the best. Its central presence would endure through times of cloud and confusion, in which it was judged only as a myth among myths or a man among men . . . however much or little our spiritual inquirers may lift the veil from their invisible kings, they will not find a vision more vivid than a man walking unveiled upon the mountains, seen of men and seeing; a visible god.[4]

Christianity is unashamedly incarnational. It proclaims that the physical, the material, the biological, is not simply something to be shaken off on the day of judgment, but something to be redeemed, restored, resurrected—for the child born on Christmas was fully God and fully man, the Savior of the world, who came to make all things new.

SCRIPTURE READING & REFLECTION

And the Word became flesh and dwelt among us, and we have seen his glory, glory as of the only Son from the Father, full of grace and truth.

JOHN 1:14

Consider the awesome reality that Christ is fully God and fully man, without it being a contradiction in terms. How does this affect the way you approach Christmas?

The invisible, unapproachable God made Himself visible and tangible in the incarnation. What does this say about God's love for you?

How might you celebrate Christmas in light of the hope of resurrection and Christ's promise to make all things new?

ON THE SIGNIFICANCE AND INSIGNIFICANCE OF RITUAL AND ROUTINE

Christmas, which the calendar assures me is coming, has been the crux of more controversies than most people remember when they take advantage of the fortunate fact that it has been so often saved from its enemies. But, like any other good thing, it has suffered much less from the heat of fanatical foes than from the coldness of frigid friends. Fanaticism only encouraged the devout to be defiant, and they resolutely repeated it as a ritual; it was much more in peril of death where people only repeated it as a routine. Now, a ritual is almost the opposite of a routine. It is because the modern world has missed that point that the modern world has in every other way fallen more and more into routine. The essence of real ritual is that a man does something because it signifies something; it may be stiff or slow or ceremonial in form; that depends on the nature of the artistic form that is used. But he does it because it is significant. It is the essence of routine that he does it because it is insignificant.

CHRISTIAN FESTIVITIES AND THE TERMITE STATE (1935)[1]

ost of us don't think of Christmas as being especially controversial. Perhaps there is an occasional objection to religious
language in association with Christmas. Perhaps there are some who
prefer the agnostic "holiday" as a blanket designation for all winter
celebrations over a word that is the conjunction of Christ and Mass.
Perhaps images of holly and wreaths are favored over images of hay
and shepherds' staffs. Perhaps songs about candy canes and silver
lanes are sung with more regularity than hymns about an incarnate
Savior. Perhaps the modern public has more of an appetite for mistletoe and holly than frankincense and myrrh.

But such objections, from a secular culture unyoked from religious
tradition, should hardly be surprising. Chesterton reminds us that
Christmas has survived such attacks in the past and will survive
such attacks in the future. What he warns us about is the attack that
comes from within: the apathy of "frigid friends." One could mention
the Puritans who disapproved of Christmas as a popish festival, or
the Pilgrims of New England, who spent their first Christmas in the
New World hewing timber rather than making merry—but they are
not the sort Chesterton is speaking of. Worse than those who refuse
to celebrate Christmas are those who celebrate it indifferently, those
for whom Christmas has become mere routine.

As a feast day celebrated by Christians for millennia, Christmas
is, by definition, a ritual. A ritual, Chesterton reminds us, "signifies something." It is a conscious, intentional observance, a deliberate
remembering. Routine, on the other hand, is more akin to muscle
memory: something we do, but without any sense of intrinsic significance behind it. When the earth-shattering reality of the incarnation
becomes merely going through the motions, when proclamations of
"peace on earth and goodwill to men" are nothing more than vague
abstractions, when our gathering and gift giving and carol singing
are no more significant than our common, day-to-day interactions, we
are in grave danger indeed. As Chesterton once observed, "There is

no mark of the immense weak-mindedness of modernity that is more striking than this general disposition to keep up old forms, but to keep them up informally and feebly. Why take something which was only meant to be respectful and preserve it disrespectfully? Why take something which you could easily abolish as a superstition and carefully perpetuate it as a bore?"[2]

At every turn, the temptation to undervalue the nonessential at the expense of the essential rears its ugly head. If we are not careful, we can allow our rituals to become routines: commonplace, comfortable, informal, feeble, boring. In Chesterton's words, "The world will never starve for want of wonders; but only for want of wonder."[3] The truth is, every day we are confronted with marvels too vast to comprehend, with beauty so astonishing we can only perceive it in part rather than in whole. Every moment of our lives should awaken us to the inestimable gift of existence. As stated in *Orthodoxy*,

> The universe is a single jewel, and while it is a natural cant[4] to talk of a jewel as peerless and priceless, of this jewel it is literally true. This cosmos is indeed without peer and without price: for there cannot be another one.[5]

As for us, may it never be said that familiarity breeds contempt. May we be unabashedly ritualistic. Audaciously traditional. May the glory of Christmas never lose its luster. May the gospel never lose its power. May we never starve for want of wonder in a world of wonders. If all the earth grows cold, may we be the ones who feast and sing and celebrate and so illuminate the surrounding darkness— for these things do, indeed, signify something.

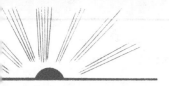

SCRIPTURE READING & REFLECTION

Let us be grateful for receiving a kingdom that cannot be shaken, and thus let us offer to God acceptable worship, with reverence and awe, for our God is a consuming fire.

HEBREWS 12:28-29

Take stock of your faith today. Has the message of the gospel lost its power for you? If so, remind yourself of the earth-shattering reality of the incarnation, of a kingdom that cannot be shaken, and assume a posture of reverence and awe before the God who is a consuming fire.

Consider some traditions you could incorporate that would increase your capacity for wonder this Christmas season.

How might you view the rituals of Christmas as truly significant and avoid falling into routine?

꒰⸝⸝ DAY 17 ⸝⸝꒱

A WORD OF GRATITUDE
TO SANTA CLAUS

As a child I was faced with a phenomenon requiring explanation. I hung up at the end of my bed an empty stocking,
which in the morning became a full stocking. I had done
nothing to produce the things that filled it. I had not worked
for them, or made them or helped to make them. I had not
even been good—far from it.

And the explanation was that a certain being whom
people called Santa Claus was benevolently disposed toward
me. . . . What we believed was that a certain benevolent
agency did give us those toys for nothing. And, as I say, I
believe it still. I have merely extended the idea.

Then I only wondered who put the toys in the stocking;
now I wonder who put the stocking by the bed, and the bed
in the room, and the room in the house, and the house on the
planet, and the great planet in the void.

Once I only thanked Santa Claus for a few dolls and
crackers. Now, I thank him for stars and street faces and wine
and the great sea. Once I thought it delightful and astonishing

to find a present so big that it only went halfway into the stocking. Now I am delighted and astonished every morning to find a present so big that it takes two stockings to hold it, and then leaves a great deal outside; it is the large and preposterous present of myself, as to the origin of which I can offer no suggestion except that Santa Claus gave it to me in a fit of peculiarly fantastic goodwill.

BLACK AND WHITE (1903)[1]

*O*ur modern conception of Santa Claus is the product of a snow-ball of traditions, which has grown in girth as it has tumbled on over the centuries. The character originated in Scandinavian mythology as *Sinterklaas*, based on the fourth-century Greek bishop Saint Nicholas, known for his liberal (and anonymous) gift giving. Chesterton describes "Saint Nicholas of Bari . . . represented in a well-known Italian picture of the later Middle Ages, not only as performing the duty of a gift-bringer, but as actually doing it by the methods of a burglar. He is represented as climbing up the grille or lattice of a house, solely in order to drop little bags of gold among the members of a poor family."[2] Over time, Saint Nicholas became Father Christmas, an elderly gentlemen with a reindeer-pulled sled who visited the homes of children at Christmas, bestowing gifts. By the seventeenth century, depictions of Father Christmas included green clothing and a brown beard. We have American advertising to thank for the bleaching of the beard and the red color of his garments.

Though some Christians view the figure of Santa Claus as a sort of "secular substitute" for Christ, Chesterton would argue that Santa is an indispensable fixture of the Christmas season. In *The Everlasting Man*, he says:

Father Christmas is not an allegory of snow and holly; he is not merely the stuff called snow afterwards artificially given a human form, like a snow man. He is something that gives a new meaning to the white world and the evergreens; so that snow itself seems to be warm rather than cold. The test therefore is purely imaginative. But imaginative does not mean imaginary. It does not follow that it is all what the moderns call subjective, when they mean false. Every true artist does feel, consciously or unconsciously, that he is touching transcendental truths; that his images are shadows of things seen through the veil. In other words, the natural mystic does know that there is something *there*; something behind the clouds or within the trees; but he believes that the pursuit of beauty is the way to find it; that imagination is a sort of incantation that can call it up.[3]

In an article from 1909, in which he laments the loss of religion in the modern world, he says, "Father Christmas was with us when the fairies departed; and please God he will still be with us when the gods return."[4] And elsewhere: "Weak things must boast of being new. . . . But strong things can boast of being old. Strong things can boast of being moribund. In the case of Christmas it is quite easy to put a simple test. All the great writers who have praised Christmas customs have praised them as antiquated customs. All the authors who have eulogised Father Christmas have eulogised him as a very elderly gentleman."[5] The figure that lives on in our traditions is largely imaginative, but he does touch "transcendental truths." He is part of a mass of "antiquated customs" associated with Christmas, of which we can say, they are not merely old, but strong. Santa Claus can make his merry rounds and fly his sleigh from house to house because Christmas is a time when the impossible is possible, when "imagination is an incantation."

When Chesterton says he is grateful to Santa Claus for life, because Santa gave it to him in "a fit of peculiarly fantastic goodwill," he is, of course, being facetious—but there is a truth behind the sentiment. If nothing else, Christmas should foster a spirit of heartfelt gratitude within us. We should, like Chesterton, not only marvel that Christmas fills the stockings at the end of our beds, but that there is a bed to hang the stocking on, a room to put the bed in, a house about the room, a planet about the house, the great void of space about the planet. Christmas—and I dare say Santa Claus—should open our hearts and minds and spirits to the gift of existence itself.

SCRIPTURE READING & REFLECTION

What do you have that you did not receive?

I CORINTHIANS 4:7

Take a moment and consider the extraordinary gift of life itself. How does this impact your sense of gratitude?

How did you think of Santa Claus when you were a child? How can you recover that childlike spirit?

Paul reminds us that all of life is a gift. How can you apply this perspective to your daily life?

ON THE ASSOCIATION BETWEEN BABIES AND STAR-SUSTAINING STRENGTH

Any agnostic or atheist whose childhood has known a real Christmas has ever afterwards, whether he likes it or not, an association in his mind between two ideas that most of mankind must regard as remote from each other; the idea of a baby and the idea of unknown strength that sustains the stars. His instincts and imagination can still connect them, when his reason can no longer see the need of the connection; for him there will always be some savor of religion about the mere picture of a mother and a baby; some hint of mercy and softening about the mere mention of the dreadful name of God. But the two ideas are not naturally or necessarily combined. . . . It has been created in our minds by Christmas because we are Christians; because we are psychological Christians even when we are not theological ones. In other words, this combination of ideas has emphatically, in the much disputed phrase, altered human nature. There is really a difference between the man who knows it and the man who does not. It may not be a difference of moral worth, for the Moslem or the Jew might be worthier according to his lights; but it is a plain fact about the crossing of two particular lights, the conjunction of two stars in our particular horoscope. Omnipotence and impotence, or divinity and infancy, do definitely make a sort of epigram which a million repetitions cannot turn into a platitude. It is not unreasonable to call it unique. Bethlehem is emphatically a place where extremes meet.

THE EVERLASTING MAN (1925)[1]

At some point or other, you have most likely heard someone refer to modern Western culture as being "post-Christian." If the meaning of the statement is merely that we live at a time in history when a large percentage of people are irreligious (or unaffiliated with a specific religion) and much of what is culturally acceptable stands in stark opposition to biblical notions of morality, then the statement can hardly be challenged.

But if ours is a post-Christian culture, it is a culture haunted by the inescapable shadow of Christianity. Our notions of human rights and the dignity of the individual are not the natural byproduct of secularism, but the fruit of a worldview that recognizes human beings as being made in the *imago Dei*. The Judeo-Christian tradition is the basis of our laws, our liberty, our justice. This is why Chesterton says "we are psychological Christians even when we are not theological ones." He expands on the idea in *Heretics*: "If any one wants to hold the end of a chain which really goes back to the heathen mysteries, he had better take hold of a festoon of flowers at Easter or a string of sausages at Christmas. Everything else in the modern world is of Christian origin, even everything that seems most anti-Christian. The French Revolution is of Christian origin. The newspaper is of Christian origin. The anarchists are of Christian origin. Physical science is of Christian origin. The attack on Christianity is of Christian origin."[2]

Take the issue of Christian imagery and symbolism. The sight of a cross—be it perched upon a steeple or strung around a neck—cannot help but conjure images of the bloodied and beaten Christ nailed to the tree, as the sight of bread and wine evokes images of the Last Supper, or the sight of a mother and child images of the first Christmas. These connotations can be consciously suppressed in various ways, but they live on in the "instincts and imagination" to the degree that "there is really a difference between the man who knows it and the man who does not." For those who have "known a real Christmas," be they theists, atheists, or anyone in between, this unexpected confluence of ideas—of a newborn child and "an unknown strength that sustains the stars"—possesses a lyrical quality that colors all notions of mother hood, in that there will "always be some savor of religion about the mere picture of a mother and a baby." This "epigram," as Chesterton describes it—of "omnipotence and impotence," of "divinity and infancy"—is more than novel; it is revolutionary. Christmas not only changed the world; it changed the way we *see* the world. It not only introduced a new chapter in the human story; it forever "altered human nature." Reality, in a very real sense, would never be the same. Our imaginations are forever baptized by the story of the incarnation.

For those of us who believe, it is, of course, more than *just* a story. In *The Everlasting Man*, Chesterton defends the Christian faith by saying that "it fits the lock . . . it is like life. It is one among many stories; only it happens to be a true story. It is one among many philosophies; only it happens to be the truth. We accept it; and the ground is solid under our feet and the road is open before us. It does not imprison us in a dream of destiny or a consciousness of the universal delusion. It opens to us not only incredible heavens but what seems to some an equally incredible earth, and makes it credible. This is the sort of truth that is hard to explain because it is a fact; but it is a fact to which we can call witnesses. We are Christians and Catholics not because we worship a key, but because we have passed a door; and felt the wind that is the trumpet of liberty blow over the land of the living."[3]

Today, let us behold, with awe and wonder, the child who is also the sustainer of stars and painter of galaxies. Let us thank God not just that such a gift should be given, but that our hearts have been opened to receive it—for "there truly is a difference between those who know it and those who do not."

SCRIPTURE READING & REFLECTION

"Where were you when I laid the foundation of the earth?

Tell me, if you have understanding.

Who determined its measurements—surely you know!

Or who stretched the line upon it?

On what were its bases sunk,

or who laid its cornerstone,

when the morning stars sang together

and all the sons of God shouted for joy?"

JOB 38:4-7

How does the knowledge that He who "laid the foundations of the earth" is He who was in the manger affect your appreciation of Christmas?

Job longed for a mediator between God and man. Reflect on the Scripture passage above in light of the knowledge that Jesus Christ was a fulfillment of that desire.

Chesterton says that while many people are "psychological Christians," fewer have "passed through the door" and "felt the wind that is the trumpet of liberty blow over the land of the living." What difference has that "experienced knowledge" made in your life?

∕⊰ DAY 19 ⊱∖

IN DEFENSE OF THE MATERIAL SUBSTANCE OF CHRISTMAS PRESENTS

A little while ago I saw a statement by Mrs. Eddy on this subject, in which she said that she did not give presents in a gross, sensuous, terrestrial sense, but sat still and thought about Truth and Purity till all her friends were much better for it. Now I do not say that this plan is either superstitious or impossible, and no doubt it has an economic charm. I say it is un-Christian in the same solid and prosaic sense that playing a tune backwards is unmusical or saying "ain't" is ungrammatical. I do not know that there is any Scriptural text or Church Council that condemns Mrs. Eddy's theory of Christmas presents: but Christianity condemns it, as soldiering condemns running away. The two attitudes are antagonistic not only in their theology, not only in their thought, but in their state of soul before they ever begin to think. The idea of embodying goodwill—that is, of putting it into a body—is the huge and primal idea of the Incarnation. A gift of God that can be seen and touched is the whole point of the epigram of the creed. Christ Himself was a Christmas present. The note of material Christmas is struck even before He is born in the first movements of the sages and the star. The Three Kings came to Bethlehem bringing gold and frankincense and myrrh. If they had only brought Truth and Purity and Love there would have been no Christian art and no Christian civilisation.

THE CONTEMPORARY REVIEW (1910)[1]

In Chesterton's day, Mrs. Eddy (the founder of the Church of Christ, Scientist) thought that contemplating truth and purity at Christmastime would be preferable to bestowing physical gifts in the "gross, sensuous, terrestrial" sense. Like Mrs. Eddy, the culture of today has a tendency to value the vague and abstract over the tangible and definitive. When someone is sick, petitions are submitted not for heartfelt prayers, but for "positive thoughts." In the modern imagination, an earnest appeal to a benevolent God is tantamount to summoning the fairy godmother. We are enlightened, civilized people, and have moved on from such superstitious nonsense. Therefore, let us offer up our positive thoughts, releasing them into the great ether, that they might float along the ocean of goodwill and perhaps find their way to the suffering soul in question (what happens at that point is anyone's guess).

But in the case of Christmas, mere positivity is not enough. However well-intentioned, Mrs. Eddy's recipe is "un-Christian in the same solid and prosaic sense that playing a tune backwards is unmusical or saying 'ain't' is ungrammatical." That's not to say that the contemplation of moral virtue is a waste of mental energy. We should contemplate such things, and contemplate them often, but all the better that we should embody them. The point of Christmas is not that it is an immaterial notion, but an incarnational fact. At Christmas, "goodwill" was manifested in the figure of Christ. Christmas is nothing less than the celebration of the tangible, physical, material, tactile presence of Immanuel: God with us. At every turn, the modern world tempts us to forget this fact. We are told that Christmas is a time of charity and love, but the charitable, loving God who offered His Son as the ultimate "Christmas present" is strangely absent from the picture. We are told that Christmas is a season of familial warmth, but He "from whom every family in heaven and on earth is named" (Eph. 3:15) is rarely named. We are told to be joyful, but the good news of the gospel of great joy is seldom proclaimed.

What Chesterton encourages us to consider is that the act of exchanging gifts at Christmas is an embodied tradition that honors the physicality of the incarnation. He argues that if the wise men "had only brought Truth and Purity and Love there would have been no Christian art and no Christian civilisation." The gifts bestowed by the wise men were of great value in the ancient world, and each, in turn, was a recognition of the identity of the child in the manger: gold symbolized His kingship, frankincense His office as high priest, myrrh His healing power (that His broken body would one day be anointed with similar spices is no coincidence). These gifts were anything but vague abstractions; they were tangible, costly offerings to the incarnate Christ. As Chesterton expresses elsewhere, these gifts indicated "that He would be crowned like a King; that He should be worshipped like a God; and that He should die like a man. And these things would sound like Eastern flattery, were it not for the third."[2]

This season, as you prepare to give (and to receive), remember that the exchange of gifts is not empty tradition, but a joyful, intentional practice acknowledging the "embodied goodwill" of Christmas. The Savior of the world is not a ghost or a phantom— though the disciples, faced with the strange reality of His resurrected body, feared that He might be. In response, Jesus said, "See my hands and my feet, that it is I myself. Touch me, and see. For a spirit does not have flesh and bones as you see that I have" (Luke 24:39). Perhaps someone would be so kind as to pass along the message to Mrs. Eddy.

SCRIPTURE READING & REFLECTION

Every good gift and every perfect gift is from above, coming down from the Father of lights, with whom there is no variation or shadow due to change.

JAMES 1:17

How can you be more thoughtful in your giving of gifts this Christmas?

How does the incarnational reality of Christmas impact your appreciation of the season?

What difference does it make that Christ is not merely spirit, but flesh and bones?

✂ DAY 20 ✎

WITH RESPECT TO
ROT, RIOT, AND RELIGION

The truth is that there is an alliance between religion and real
fun, of which the modern thinkers have never got the key,
and which they are quite unable to criticize or to destroy. All
Socialist Utopias, all new pagan Paradises, promised in this age
to mankind have all one horrible fault. They are all dignified.
. . . But being undignified is the essence of all real happiness,
whether before God or man. Hilarity involves humility; nay,
it involves humiliation. . . . Religion is much nearer to riotous
happiness than it is to the detached and temperate types of
happiness in which gentlemen and philosophers find their
peace. Religion and riot are very near, as the history of all
religions proves. Riot means being a rotter; and religion means
knowing you are a rotter.

THE ILLUSTRATED LONDON NEWS (1907)[1]

The truth of the matter is, it is impossible to take Christmas seriously while taking yourself seriously. Chesterton says, "there is an alliance between religion and real fun"—but in God's kingdom, mortification always precedes exaltation. Preceding the fun is a startling humiliation. The first are last, the last first. The weak are strong. The poor are rich. The meek inherit the land. "Humility was largely meant as a restraint upon the arrogance and infinity of the appetite of man," Chesterton says in *Orthodoxy*. "A man was meant to be doubtful about himself, but undoubting about the truth; this has been exactly reversed. Nowadays the part of a man that a man does assert is exactly the part he ought not to assert—himself. The part he doubts is exactly the part he ought not to doubt—the Divine Reason."[2] As he expresses in his epic poem *The Ballad of the White Horse*:

Pride juggles with her toppling towers,
They strike the sun and cease,
But the firm feet of humility
They grip the ground like trees.[3]

The "pagan paradises" prophesied by the modern world are citadels to a dignified (one might say *deified*) humanity, intent on building towers to heaven. But what if "being undignified is the essence of all real happiness"? What if "hilarity involves . . . humiliation"? What if those searching for peace through "detached and temperate types of happiness" have missed true and abiding joy? What if real fun is found not in ever-expanding conquest but in full-scale surrender?

If Christmas is not an offense to your dignity, if it does not lay waste to your pride, you have not known Christmas in all its humbling glory. If the Son of God "did not count equality with God a thing to be grasped, but emptied himself, by taking the form of a servant, being born in the likeness of men" (Phil. 2:5-7), then it stands to reason that we have no place to stand. Like Isaiah, we must recognize the uncleanness of our lips; like John, we must fall down as dead in the presence of a holy God. Humility means not just that we are unworthy, but that we know we are. Many people are "riotous rotters," but "religion means *knowing* you are a rotter"—being painfully aware of your own weakness, sinfulness, brokenness. But thanks be to God, we are not *only* unqualified sinners, but unqualified sinners saved by His mercy, and His mercy alone. "For all have sinned and fall short of the glory of God, and are justified by his grace as a gift" (Rom. 3:23–24a).

In the early 1900s, an editor at *The Times* asked the following question of several well-known authors: "What's wrong with the world today?" Chesterton responded:

> *Dear Sir,*
> *I am.*
> *Yours, G.K. Chesterton*[4]

Only a humble man, fully aware of his own sinfulness and his dire need for mercy, could respond in such a way. It should come as no surprise that Chesterton loved Christmas, because Christmas itself is an unmerited gift to a world of undeserving rotters. It is a liberating blow to the ego, a merciful gut punch to the hubristic spirit. It levels the playing field, flattens hierarchies, brings the proudest among us to their knees. Only in humble contriteness can we approach the throne of grace and partake of the "riotous happiness" of union with God. As Chesterton says in the conclusion to *Orthodoxy*, "Joy, which was the small publicity of the pagan, is the gigantic secret of the Christian." He goes on to speak of Christ as having concealed something: "there was in that shattering personality a thread that must be called shyness. There was something that He hid from all men when He went up a mountain to pray. There was something that He covered constantly by abrupt silence or impetuous isolation.

There was some one thing that was too great for God to show us when He walked upon our earth; and I have sometimes fancied that it was His mirth."[5]

SCRIPTURE READING & REFLECTION

"For everyone who exalts himself will be humbled, and he who humbles himself will be exalted."

LUKE 14:11

What would it look like for you to fully surrender to God this season? What is He asking you to let go of? What is He asking you to embrace?

How might you approach Christmas with the humility of a reverent worshiper rather than a selfish consumer?

Consider the mirth of God at work in the "good news" and "great joy" of Christmas. Think of some ways you can share the "riotous happiness" of God with others this Christmas.

AS TO THE UNCOMFORTABLE COMFORT OF CHRISTMAS

Being happy is not so important as having a jolly time.
Philosophers are happy; saints have a jolly time. The
important thing in life is not to keep a steady system of
pleasure and composure (which can be done quite well by
hardening one's heart or thickening one's head), but to keep
alive in oneself the immortal power of astonishment and
laughter, and a kind of young reverence. This is why religion
always insists on special days like Christmas, while philosophy
always tends to despise them. Religion is interested not in
whether a man is happy, but whether he is still alive, whether
he can still react in a normal way to new things, whether he
blinks in a blinding light or laughs when he is tickled. That
is the best of Christmas, that it is a startling and disturbing
happiness; it is an uncomfortable comfort.

THE ILLUSTRATED LONDON NEWS (1907)[1]

hat does it mean to be alive? Not alive in the literal sense of being a living, breathing, thinking thing—for one can live and breathe and think in despair. One can chase after pleasure and happiness only to find, in the end, vanity and striving after wind (Eccl. 1:14). Chesterton reminds us that happiness is not synonymous with vitality, that a meager pulse in the vein is not synonymous with true life. In his estimation, anyone can be happy (he uses the term *philosophers*, but then we are all, at some level, philosophers), but only saints can be jolly, for "religion is interested not in whether a man is happy, but whether he is still alive."

By Chesterton's definition, to be jolly is to walk in the joy of the Lord. Joy, as defined by Scripture, is not blind optimism or manufactured cheer; it is not freedom from pain or sorrow (in fact, godly joy is often found in the midst of trial), but a secure and abiding hope—for our God is in the business of making all things new (Rev. 21:5). He who began a good work in us will bring it to completion at the day of Christ Jesus (Phil. 1:6). The earth will be full of the knowledge of the Lord as the waters cover the sea (Isa. 11:9). Sorrow and sighing will flee away (Isa. 35:10). He will wipe every tear from our eyes. Death will be no more. The former things will pass away (Rev. 7:17).

In light of this hope of glory (Rom. 5:2), we have permission to be unapologetically jolly. Unabashedly joyful. Unflaggingly hopeful. We can live each day to the fullest—not by means of "hardening one's heart" or "thickening one's head"—but because in Christ we have found life, abundant and overflowing.

Chesterton once said that "thanks are the highest form of thought; and that gratitude is happiness doubled by wonder."[2] The unfortunate reality is that while many people might "keep a steady system of pleasure and composure," they might know fleeting moments of contentment, occasional sensations of gratitude—a deeper joy evades them. "[Dante] Rossetti makes the remark somewhere, bitterly but with great truth, that the worst moment for the atheist is when he is really thankful and has nobody to thank."[3]

But let's be honest: precious few of us are the jolly saints Chesterton describes. Many of us have allowed parts of ourselves to calcify, to deaden, so that we no longer know how to "keep ourselves alive with a kind of young reverence." Many of us have lost the eyes to see and the ears to hear. If Christmas has lost its power to startle and disturb you, if you no longer find the bewildering claims of the incarnation uncomfortable, then Chesterton invites you to rediscover Christmas in all its startling, disturbing, uncomfortable splendor.

Today, may we allow Christmas to wake us from the dead, to shock us out of apathy, to rouse us from calcified faith and stagnant joy. May we taste life, abundant and overflowing. May we rediscover "the immortal power of astonishment and laughter," the gratitude that is "happiness doubled by wonder," and so discover "the best of Christmas." For God's sake, may we be jolly.

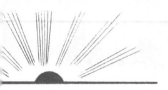

SCRIPTURE READING & REFLECTION

"The thief comes only to steal and kill and destroy. I came that they may have life and have it abundantly."

JOHN 10:10

Take an honest account of your life. Is it the abundant life Jesus talked about? If not, ask Him to rouse you from calcified faith and stagnant joy.

Take an account of all the nonmaterial blessings in your life. Consider how you might approach Christmas with a greater degree of gratitude this year.

How might you keep yourself in a state of "young reverence" this Christmas season?

10

H

⸙ **DAY 22** ⸙

OF BARBARIANS, PHILOSOPHERS, AND A CAVE OF DREAMS

The barbarian who conceived the crudest fancy about the sun being stolen and hidden in a box, or the wildest myth about the god being rescued and his enemy deceived with a stone, was nearer to the secret of the cave and knew more about the crisis of the world than all those in the circle of cities round the Mediterranean who had become content with cold abstractions or cosmopolitan generalisations; than all those who were spinning thinner and thinner threads of thought out of the transcendentalism of Plato or the orientalism of Pythagoras. The place that the shepherds found was not an academy or an abstract republic; it was not a place of myths allegorised or dissected or explained or explained away. It was a place of dreams come true. Since that hour no mythologies have been made in the world. Mythology is a search.

THE EVERLASTING MAN (1925)[1]

t hand is the issue of *philosophy*. Specifically, a philosophy of life, a worldview. Both the "barbarian" and the learned men "in the circle of the cities round the Mediterranean" were philoso-phers; they both attempted, in varying ways, to make sense of the world. But in attempting to make sense of the world, one should consider what world one is making sense of. "A cosmic philosophy is not constructed to fit a man," Chesterton says elsewhere. "A cosmic philosophy is constructed to fit a cosmos."[2] The cosmos we inhabit, the cosmos Chesterton beheld through his enchanted intellect, has a way of resisting our erudite postulations and ten dollar words—though we formulate "cold abstractions" and "cosmopolitan general-isations" and "spin threads of thought" based on the teachings of Plato or Pythagoras or any number of modern sages, gurus, or crack-pots. Much like ancient Athens, our modern culture is a marketplace of ideas (and idols). We are in dire need of an apostle Paul to come along and point out the God we've been grasping for unaware. In Chesterton's words, "St. Paul said that the Greeks had one altar to an unknown god. But in truth all their gods were unknown gods. And the real break in history did come when St. Paul declared to them whom they had ignorantly worshipped."[3]

Chesterton encourages us to behold with fresh eyes the strange, enchanted universe that is the setting of the human story. As he says in *Orthodoxy*,

> The only words that ever satisfied me as describing Nature
> are the terms used in the fairy books, "charm," "spell,"
> "enchantment." They express the arbitrariness of the fact and
> its mystery. A tree grows fruit because it is a magic tree. Water
> runs downhill because it is bewitched. The sun shines because
> it is bewitched. I deny altogether that this is fantastic or even
> mystical . . . this fairy-tale language about things is simply
> rational and agnostic.[4]

The God-breathed world we inhabit is a *magical* place, charged with enigmatic beauty. Behold the cave in ancient Judea—a cave found by shepherds, fresh from the hilltop and smelling of mud and grass—a cave which, for a short time, was home to the world's greatest secret. The incarnation, Chesterton suggests, was the realization of a dream—the dream of a purpose beyond the stars, of gods and demigods and magic and mystery, of sacrifice and supplication. The incarnation tells us that the universe is not a meaningless void. It tells us that hope and love are not mere abstractions. It tells us that our longing for meaning and purpose and beauty is not in vain. It tells us that, in the end, we will, somehow, live happily ever after. The myth had, as C. S. Lewis put it, somehow become a fact. It was the True Myth to end all myths.[5] "Since that hour no mythologies have been made in the world."

The question Chesterton poses is this: What is true knowledge? Could it be that man in his most primal existence, chicken-scratching on the walls of caves and searching for pictures in the stars, was somehow closer to the "crisis of the world" than the learned and civilized could ever be? Could it be that common people, weaned on nursery tales and simple songs, possess a capacity for faith that is seldom found in the halls of the wise? After all, it was not the learned but shepherds who first found Christ in the cave; and when the wise men of the East arrived, they came not to pontificate, but to bow. This Christmas, let us join them, as we draw near to "the mystery hidden for ages and generations but now revealed to his saints" (Col. 1:26), in "a place of dreams come true."

SCRIPTURE READING & REFLECTION

Let no one deceive himself. If anyone among you thinks that he is wise in this age, let him become a fool that he may become wise. For the wisdom of this world is folly with God.

I CORINTHIANS 3:18-19

According to Scripture, what is true wisdom?

How might you trade worldly wisdom for the "foolishness" of the gospel?

How might you, like the wise men, put aside your own understanding to bow at the feet of Jesus this Christmas season?

TO MARRY, BE MERRY, AND MAKE MERRY

Christmas, like so many other Christian and Catholic creations, is a wedding. It is the wedding of the wilder spirit of human enjoyment with the higher spirit of humility and the mystical sense. And the parallel of a wedding holds good in more ways than one; because this new danger which threatens Christmas is the same that has long vulgarised and vitiated weddings. It is quite right that there should be pomp and popular rejoicing at a wedding; I do not in the least agree with those who would have it a purely private and personal thing like a proposal or engagement. If a man is not proud of getting married, what is he proud of, and why in the name of nonsense is he getting married at all? But in the normal way all this merry-making is subordinate to the marriage; because it is *in honour* of the marriage. People came there to be married and not to be merry; and they are merry because they did. But in the snobbish society wedding the serious purpose is entirely lost sight of, and nothing remains but frivolity. For frivolity is trying to rejoice with nothing to rejoice over. The result is that at last

even the frivolity as frivolity begins to fail. People who began
by coming together only for fun end by doing it only for
fashion; and there is no more even of faint suggestion of fun
but only of fuss.

G.K.'S WEEKLY (1925)[1]

Jesus not only attended weddings, He performed His first public
miracle at a wedding (it is no coincidence that it involved wine,
a symbol of festive celebration). In the book of Isaiah, the prophet
waxes eloquent about a sumptuous banquet on the mountain of God
—"a feast of rich food, a feast of well-aged wine, of rich food full of
marrow, of aged wine well refined" (Isa. 25:6). Throughout Scripture,
marriage is used as a symbol of God's relationship with His people:
He is the husband, we are the bride. The grand narrative of the Bible
begins with a wedding and ends with a wedding feast.

Chesterton speaks of Christmas as a "wedding of the wilder spirit
of human enjoyment with the higher spirit of humility and the mystical sense" and goes on to say the "the parallel of a wedding holds
good in more ways than one"—for Christmas is not just a ritual, but
a revelry. At a wedding, the "merry-making" is "subordinate to the
marriage; because it is *in honour* of the marriage." The marriage is the
purpose of the gathering; the revelry is the natural result thereof:
"People came there to be married and not to be merry; and they are
merry because they did." If we lose sight of why we have gathered
in the first place, our revelry becomes frivolity, which Chesterton
defines as "trying to rejoice with nothing to rejoice over."

In the modern world, Christmas has a tendency to be treated
like the "snobbish society wedding" Chesterton describes: it has
all the marks of a grand celebration, but with nothing definitive to
celebrate. Fun gives way to mere fashion and fuss. The traditions
are upheld because they are nostalgic and enjoyable, but we have

forgotten why they were worth celebrating in the first place. We have found ourselves at the wedding reception, and have forgotten about the wedding that preceded it.

If the child born on Christmas was no more significant than any other child born at any other time and place, if the star the shepherds followed was nothing more than an astrological coincidence, then Christmas is not worth celebrating at all. As Chesterton once said,

> Frivolity does not come from the frivolous. It does not come from those who are allowed a holiday. It comes too evidently from those who are not allowed a holiday. It comes from those laborious unfortunates for whom Christmas is not Christmas. It is not a product of the observance of the Christmas spirit, but a product of its violation.[2]

Modernity is largely the story of human beings attempting to find significance apart from God—in pride, pleasure, or any number of self-directed pursuits. As Chesterton says, "Man has always lost his way. He has been a tramp ever since Eden; but he always knew, or thought he knew, what he was looking for. . . . But in the bleak and blinding hail of skepticism to which he has been now so long sub- jected, he has begun for the first time to be chilled, not merely in his hopes, but in his desires. For the first time in history he begins really to doubt the object of his wanderings on the earth. He has always lost his way; but now he has lost his address."[3]

By God's grace, may we never forget our address. May we never be so unfortunate as to find ourselves attempting to rejoice with noth- ing to rejoice over. May we remember that we celebrate Christmas because there is something definitive to celebrate—and that the wedding precedes the reception. May we feast and make merry as we anticipate the great feast at the end of the age.

SCRIPTURE READING & REFLECTION

Then I heard what seemed to be the voice of a great multitude, like the roar of many waters and like the sound of mighty peals of thunder, crying out,

> "Hallelujah!
> For the Lord our God
>   the Almighty reigns.
> Let us rejoice and exult
>   and give him the glory,
> for the marriage of the Lamb has come,
>   and his Bride has made herself ready;
> it was granted her to clothe herself
>   with fine linen, bright and pure"—

for the fine linen is the righteous deeds of the saints.

REVELATION 19:6-8

Think back on some weddings you have attended. Consider how your Christmas celebration might reflect Chesterton's idea of Christmas as a "wedding of the wilder spirit of human enjoyment with the higher spirit of humility and the mystical sense."

How might you wholeheartedly rejoice this Christmas season?

How might your anticipation of the marriage supper of the Lamb affect your observance of the holidays?

IN REGARD TO THE ANCIENT SYMBOL OF THE FLAME

All ceremony depends on symbol; and all symbols have been vulgarised and made stale by the commercial conditions of our time. . . . Of all these faded and falsified symbols, the most melancholy example is the ancient symbol of the flame. In every civilised age and country, it has been a natural thing to talk of some great festival on which "the town was illuminated." There is no meaning nowadays in saying that the town was illuminated. There is no point or purpose in having it illuminated for any normal and noble enthusiasm, such as the winning of a victory or the granting of a charter. The whole town is illuminated already, but not for noble things. It is illuminated solely to insist on the immense importance of trivial and material things, blazoned from motives entirely mercenary. . . . It is no good to send up a golden and purple rocket for the glory of the King and Country, or to light a red and raging bonfire on the day of St. George, when everybody is used to seeing the same fiery alphabet proclaiming the importance of Tibble's Tooth Paste or Giggle's Chewing Gum.

The new illumination has not, indeed, made Tibble and Giggle so important as St. George and King George; because nothing could. But it has made people weary of the way of proclaiming great things, by perpetually using it to proclaim small things. It has not destroyed the difference between light and darkness, but it has allowed the lesser light to put out the greater.

THE ILLUSTRATED LONDON NEWS (1927)[1]

We live in an age of relentless distractions. We are inundated with endless news feeds and celebrity gossip, a glut of enter-tainment options, a deluge of cursory amusements and superficial diversions. If Chesterton lamented the loss of "the ancient symbol of the flame" in an age where firelight was superfluous, where every town was illuminated with "fiery alphabets" proclaiming the impor-tance of unimportant things, then we have taken the "proclamation of small things" to new heights. At every turn, there is the tempta-tion to overvalue the insignificant and undervalue the significant, to champion the insubstantial at the expense of the substantial. In Chesterton's words, "There is nothing [stranger] today than the importance of unimportant things. Except, of course, the unimpor-tance of important things."[2]

We see this dynamic at play in the increasing secularization of Christian holidays. Easter, a celebration of the astonishing reality of the resurrection, is reduced to a springtime carnival of pastel colors, bunnies, and candy. An egg is not so much a receptacle for new life as a receptacle for chocolate. A stone is rolled away only to better get at the treat behind it.

Christmas, likewise, has largely been stripped of its religious connotations in the modern world. The imagery of the manger, of angels, hay, and halos, has been supplanted with the more agnos-tic iconography of Santa Claus, reindeer, and sleighs (though, as we have established, Chesterton fearlessly defends Father Christmas as a Christian saint). The issue is not so much in the association, but in the organization. That a feast observed for millennia should adopt new traditions along the way is hardly surprising. New revelries must be invented, new songs sung—so long as the purpose of the feast remains. God forbid anyone should be found in some distant corner of the party, watching with furrowed brow as the candles on the cake are lit, unaware of whose birthday it is. As Chesterton once said, "The great majority of people will go on observing forms that cannot be explained; they will keep Christmas Day with Christmas gifts and Christmas benedictions; they will continue to do it; and some day suddenly wake up and discover why."[3] At least, one can hope that they will.

Modern thought, in Chesterton's words, is like a fellow who has failed "at the high jump because he had not gone far enough back for his run. . . . It is so confident of where it is going to that it does not know where it comes from."[4] Well, Christmas knows where it comes from, even if others have forgotten. It is a feast precisely because there is something worth feasting about. That thing must be primary and other things secondary. As Chesterton writes in his poem "A Christmas Carol":

And all the flowers looked up at Him
And all the stars looked down.[5]

Give Santa Claus a place at Christmas, so long as it is not the highest place. Sing songs about flying reindeer, but let them fly lower than the angels. Set cookies and milk out on Christmas Eve, but remember that flour and sugar and cream are of lesser value than gold and frankincense and myrrh. String colored lights on every house, hang them from every tree, so long as they are lesser lights, and the greater light of the ancient flame burns brighter still.

SCRIPTURE READING & REFLECTION

In him was life, and the life was the light of men. The light shines in the darkness, and the darkness has not overcome it.

JOHN 1:4-5

Consider some ways you have allowed "lesser lights" to put out "greater ones" in your life. Turn your heart to Christ, who is the life and light of men (John 1:4).

Think of your Christmas traditions as a series of concentric circles. Is Christ in the middle?

How can you quiet your heart and focus on Christ this Christmas?

⚜ DAY 25 ⚜

OF SECRETS,
DIVINE CAPS, AND
CELESTIAL POST OFFICES

Christmas, down to its most homely and even comic observances of stockings and boxes, is penetrated with this personal
idea of a secret between God and man—a divine cap that fits
the particular human head. The cosmos is conceived as a central
and celestial post-office. The postal system is, indeed, vast and
rapid, but the parcels are all addressed, sealed and inviolate.
A pillar-box is only public in order that a letter may be private.
Christmas presents are a standing protest on behalf of giving
as distinct from that mere sharing that modern moralities offer
as equivalent or superior. Christmas stands for this superb
and sacred paradox: that it is a higher spiritual transaction for
Tommy and Molly each to give each other sixpence than for
both equally to share a shilling. Christmas is something better
than a thing for all; it is a thing for everybody.

THE CONTEMPORARY REVIEW (1910)[1]

In this brief excerpt, Chesterton fires off various metaphors in such quick succession that it's easy to miss the potency of what he is saying. Let us take them each in turn:

First, he suggests that Christmas is, in its own way, "a secret between God and man"—a secret that fits the human experience like "a divine cap that fits the particular human head." The cap fits the head because the cosmos fits the head. It is not just that Christmas (and Christianity) provides a persuasive explanation for the world as it is, but that it is an explanation so illuminating that it fits the world as snugly as a hat on the crown of the head. As Chesterton says in *Orthodoxy*, "The more I saw of the merely abstract arguments against the Christian cosmology the less I thought of them. I mean that having found the moral atmosphere of the Incarnation to be common sense, I then looked at the established intellectual arguments against the Incarnation and found them to be common nonsense."[2]

Second, this "secret between God and man" is something like a "celestial post-office." A mailbox is public only so far as it conceals that which is private: letters and parcels "addressed, sealed and inviolate." The "stockings and boxes" of Christmas are symbols of the secret at the heart of the Christmas story: that Christ is a gift from God to man, an answer to the deepest longings of the human heart, a response to queries stamped and sealed and sent off into the void of space and time. As Chesterton says in *The Everlasting Man*,

> The sanity of the world was restored and the soul of man offered salvation by something which did indeed satisfy the two warring tendencies of the past; which had never been satisfied in full and most certainly never satisfied together. It met the mythological search for romance by being a story and the philosophical search for truth by being a true story. . . . The more deeply we think of the matter the more we shall conclude that, if there be indeed a God, his creation

could hardly have reached any other culmination than this granting of a real romance to the world.[3]

Third, he argues that "Christmas presents are a standing protest on behalf of giving as distinct from that of sharing." Sharing is a noble practice and should by all means be encouraged, but let us be careful not to confuse sharing with giving. Giving requires something of the giver in a way that sharing does not. Sharing is based on equality, giving on inequality (as Chesterton puts it, "charity certainly means one of two things—pardoning unpardonable acts, or loving unlovable people"[4]). That is why he says it is a "higher spiritual transaction" for two children to give each other sixpence than to share a shilling (twelve pence). "Christmas is something better than a thing for all; it is a thing for everybody." In pondering the Christian virtues, Chesterton eventually came to the conclusion that "the chief aim of that order was to give room for good things to run wild."[5] If Christ "came not to be served but to serve, and to give his life as a ransom for many" (Matt. 20:28), then we have no excuse not to "run wild" with our generosity—"not reluctantly or under compulsion" (2 Cor. 9:6–7)—but because we ourselves are the beneficiaries of unmerited grace.

This Christmas, let us marvel that the gift of Christ is truly a gift that "fits" the hunger of the human heart; an answer to our deepest desires; a sealed, inviolate parcel addressed to the whole world and to each one of us; a miracle "for all and for everybody."

SCRIPTURE READING & REFLECTION

"When you give a feast, invite the poor, the crippled, the lame, the blind, and you will be blessed, because they cannot repay you. For you will be repaid at the resurrection of the just."

LUKE 14:13-14

Consider the idea of Christmas as a "secret between God and man." How is Christmas an answer to the deepest longings of your heart?

Meditate on the idea that in Christ, God has "granted a real romance to the world."

How can you practice godly charity this Christmas season, expecting nothing in return?

ᴊᴄ᷄ DAY 26 ᷄ᴄᴊ

CONCERNING THE ENDURING FORTITUDE OF CHRISTMAS

We are constantly reminded, especially by those stunted skeptics who seem never to get beyond one step in thought, that many of the popular customs of Christmas are pagan things. . . . What these people do not see is this rather interesting fact; that if these things are pagan, they are things that have survived paganism. It is not unlikely that they will survive modernism. It is quite conceivable that they will survive industrialism or capitalism or that Socialism which is the child of capitalism. But it does not occur to these skeptics to consider the further force of their own argument. If these traditions were so tough that they survived so tremendous an upheaval as the change of the whole religion of Europe, the downfall of the universal Empire and the rise of the universal Church, it seems not impossible that they may survive a few electric fittings and a few fumbling and inefficient Education Acts. If these old human carnivals were strong enough to make a compromise with the flaming missionary of the first days of the Church, ready to be rent in pieces or roasted alive

rather than deny a detail of the creed, it seems possible that
the same human instinct might be strong enough to cope
with the poor badgered and bewildered modern elementary
schoolmaster, with no creed and ten contradictory codes,
told to read the Bible without reference to religion, and to
teach children in school to obey their parents while fining the
parents for wanting them at home.

THE ILLUSTRATED LONDON NEWS (1921)[1]

We return, once again, to the concept of Christmas as a pagan
holiday. Here, Chesterton makes the crucial observation that
Christmas did not merely borrow certain traditions from paganism;
it *survived* paganism. It was a stronger thing than all the pagan world
could offer. It was fiercer than its creeds, more potent than its rituals. As he says in *Heretics*, "The pagan set out, with admirable sense,
to enjoy himself. By the end of his civilization he had discovered that
a man cannot enjoy himself and continue to enjoy anything else."[2] In
The Everlasting Man, he writes, "A void was made by the vanish-
ing world of the whole mythology of mankind, which would have
asphyxiated like a vacuum if it had not been filled with theology."[3]
That being said, there was a moment when "Christians were invited
to set up the image of Jesus side by side with the image of Jupiter, of
Mithras, of Osiris, of Atys, or of Ammon. It was the refusal of the
Christians that was the turning-point of history."[4]

Not only did Christianity survive paganism; it has survived
humanity. If the church could endure ages of persecution, in which
missionaries were "ready to be rent in pieces or roasted alive rather
than deny a detail of the creed," if it could withstand "so tremendous an upheaval as the change of the whole religion of Europe" and
"the downfall of the universal Empire"—it stands to reason that it
will survive even modernism, industrialism, socialism, capitalism, or

anything else the human race will throw in its way. "Christendom has had a series of revolutions and in each one of them Christianity has died. Christianity has died many times and risen again; for it had a God who knew the way out of the grave."[5]

Christmas is a standing reminder of the enduring fortitude of the Christian faith: "the Merry Christmas is not slowing dying, but slowly reviving; and may stand up as one risen from the dead."[6] If the martyrs of the church could withstand torture and death in the name of Christ, counting it joy to suffer for His name, might Christmas withstand the torturous logic of modernity?

In an article from 1908, Chesterton offers the following example:

> Supposing that your father and grandfather and great-grandfather and great-great-grandfather had all left it on record that the sun in the sky was growing smaller before their very eyes, then I think we should not believe it; not because we are any wiser than they, but because if that had been the exact truth there would not by this time be any sun at all. So that when we find our fathers perpetually saying age after age that religion is dying, that religious festivity is dying, that the hearty human customs are dying, I think we are justified in saying that they were mistaken, not in their praise, but in their despair. The truth was that religion, being really a good thing, could thrive as a continual failure.[7]

If Christmas is a failure, it is a thriving failure. If it is dead, it is only for a moment. It will rise again, like a phoenix from the ashes—for it has a God who knows the way out of the grave. The sun, for a time, might be obscured by cloud and rain—but it is still in the sky. Whatever the future holds, we can be assured that Christmas will endure.

SCRIPTURE READING & REFLECTION

So the church throughout all Judea and Galilee and Samaria had peace and was being built up. And walking in the fear of the Lord and in the comfort of the Holy Spirit, it multiplied.

ACTS 9:31

Consider how the early church multiplied. How can you apply this to your walk with God?

How is Christmas a reminder of the "enduring fortitude" of the faith?

The church has survived ages of paganism, persecution, and moral darkness. How can this help you face the future with hope?

~ DAY 27 ~

WITH RESPECT TO PUDDING, CURRENCY, AND THE BETRAYAL OF CHRISTMAS

The little boy expects to find sixpences in the pudding; and this is right enough, so long as the sixpences are secondary to the pudding. Now the change from the medieval to the modern world might be very truly described under that image. It is all the difference between putting sixpences in a Christmas pudding and erecting a Christmas pudding round sixpences. There was money in the old days of Christmas and Christendom; there was merchandise; there were merchants. But the moral scheme of all the old order, whatever its other vices and diseases, always assumed that money was secondary to substance; that the merchant was secondary to the maker. . . . With the rise of the merchant adventurers the whole world gradually changed, until the preponderance was all the other way. The world was dominated by what the late Lord Birkenhead described as "the glittering prizes," without which, as he appeared to believe, men could not be really moved to any healthy or humane activity. And it is true that men came to think too much about prizes, and too little about pudding. This, in connection with ordinary pudding, is a fallacy; in connection with Christmas pudding it is a blasphemy. For there is truly something of perversity, not unmixed with profanity, about the notion of trade completely transforming a tradition of such sacred origin. Millions of perfectly healthy and worthy men and women still keep Christmas, and do in all sincerity keep it holy as well as happy. But there are some, profiting by such natural schemes of play and pleasure-seeking, who have used it for things far baser than either pleasure-seeking or play. They have betrayed Christmas. For them the substance of Christmas, like the substance of Christmas pudding, has become stale stuff in which their own treasure is buried; and they have only multiplied the sixpences into thirty pieces of silver.

THE ILLUSTRATED LONDON NEWS (1933)[1]

The tradition of hiding sixpence in Christmas pudding traces back to the time of Queen Victoria (as the story goes, her husband, Prince Albert, introduced the tradition to the Brits).[2] A week before Advent, Christmas pudding would be prepared and a silver sixpence coin would be hidden in the mix. Once steamed, the pudding would be stored until Christmas Day, at which time it would be divided (and promptly devoured) between members of the household. Whoever found the sixpence in their piece would be blessed with luck and good fortune for the following year. Chesterton suggests that this image of a child (in age or disposition) searching for the coin in the pudding provides a picture of "the change from the medieval to the modern world." In the old order, a child would diligently dismantle his or her pudding in search of the coin, but the coin was always understood to be secondary to the pudding itself. "Money was secondary to substance," "the merchant was secondary to the maker." But the modern world has inverted the image, "erecting a Christmas pudding around sixpence." Financial gain has become the driving motivation not just behind Christmas but also the vast majority of human effort, to the point that we cannot imagine being "moved to any healthy or humane activity" without "glittering prizes" as the end result.

It is no secret that the Christmas season means big business. The rule of commerce says, so long as people uphold traditions, they will pay for them. Unless you have the luxury of tramping through the woods at your leisure to gather mistletoe, you will pay for it by weight. Unless you are blessed with an easily accessible fir tree, an able axe, and an able body, you will pay for a tree by height. Unless you are an artisan with an elven workshop, you will purchase gifts at market value. To be fair, people must make a living. Some shrewd visionary will profit from the sale of Christmas ornaments in the shape of hamburgers or chocolates in the shape of reindeer. All well and good, so long as the "accidental or adventurous gain" does not overshadow "the idea of normal owning or enjoying." When "glittering prizes" become the motivating factor at Christmas, when the single coin is of more value than the entire pudding, it is not just a mockery of Christmas; it is a betrayal of Christmas, a "blasphemy"—"for there is truly something of perversity, not unmixed with profanity, about the notion of trade completely transforming a tradition of such sacred origin."

Elsewhere, Chesterton points out that "the Christmas season is domestic; and for that reason most people now prepare for it by struggling in tramcars, standing in queues, rushing away in trains, crowding despairingly into tea-shops, and wondering when or whether they will ever get home. I do not know whether some of them disappear for ever in the toy department or simply lie down and die in the tea-rooms; but by the look of them, it is quite likely. Just before the great festival of the home the whole population seems to have become homeless."[3] That many of us should anticipate with mounting dread the relentless busyness of the Christmas season only further proves his point. Trade has, indeed, transformed the sacred tradition of Christmas. "Modern commercial complexity eats out the heart of the thing, while actually leaving the painted shell of it."[4] Greed threatens to poison tradition, to make it merely a means to an end; to make Christmas pudding merely "stale stuff in which treasure is buried."

It is inevitable that some will use Christmas for personal gain. Some will blaspheme it. Some will betray it. Some will "multiply sixpence into thirty pieces of silver," but in the end they will be left not with a real Christmas, but merely a painted shell of it. As for the rest of us, may we keep Christmas with sincerity, may we "keep it holy as well as happy," and may we never lose sight of the forest of pudding for the glinting silver in the trees.

SCRIPTURE READING & REFLECTION

"One who is faithful in a very little is also faithful in much, and one who is dishonest in a very little is also dishonest in much. If then you have not been faithful in the unrighteous wealth, who will entrust to you the true riches? And if you have not been faithful in that which is another's, who will give you that which is your own? No servant can serve two masters, for either he will hate the one and love the other, or he will be devoted to the one and despise the other. You cannot serve God and money."

LUKE 16:10-13

What are "true riches," according to Jesus? Is He speaking of physical riches or spiritual riches?

How can you remember that "the sixpence is secondary to the pudding" this Christmas?

Think of how you might resist "the relentless busyness" of an overcommercialized Christmas.

✣ DAY 28 ✣

CONCERNING THE LIBERAL AND CONSERVATIVE BALANCE OF CHRISTMAS

It is self-evident at first sight that Christmas is both conservative and liberal, so long as we have the sense to avoid capital letters for the two words. It would be nothing if it did not conserve the traditions of our fathers; it would be nothing if it did not give with liberality to our brethren. Keeping Christmas at all involves the admission that England has already valuable and honourable traditions of a local and domestic sort. Helping the poor at Christmas at all involves in itself the admission that England does not possess a satisfactory economic distribution, that all is not well, or anything like well, with England. In other words, Christmas, being a Christian institution, contains in itself already the two alternative actions towards society—the preservation of what is good in the past, the removal of what is bad in the present.

THE ILLUSTRATED LONDON NEWS (1923)[1]

A real Christmas, Chesterton reminds us, is both liberal in its charity and conservative in its traditions. While we may "have the sense to avoid capital letters for the two words," the truth of the matter is, there is an indisputable political dimension to Christmas, as there is a political dimension to Christianity. If Christ is King—if "of the increase of his government and of peace there will be no end" (Isa. 9:7), if "the earth will be filled with the knowledge of the glory of the LORD" (Hab. 2:14), if "the kingdom of the world has become the kingdom of our Lord" (Rev. 11:15)—then His kingship lays claim to every nation, every throne, every square inch of man's domain.

Christmas is a foretaste of the new creation, for it "contains in itself . . . the two alternative actions towards society—the preservation of what is good in the past, the removal of what is bad in the present." In Chesterton's words, "there is just this difference between the decay of religious things like Christmas and the decay of merely worldly things like the Party System—that we know of worldly things that when they die they are dead, and that is exactly what we do not know about religious things: Man is so made that a bad religion may last longer than a good Government; just as (barring accidents) the weaker head lasts longer than the hardest hat. If Christmas were actually as bad a thing as it is really a good thing, the mere utilitarians and rationalists would find it almost equally impossible to root it out. If Santa Claus did not come down the chimney from heaven, but up the coal-hole from quite a different place, it would still be almost equally difficult to barricade a European house against him. The facts melt and alter perpetually; it is the fancies that endure."[2]

The charity of Christmas is something stronger and altogether different from the "unsatisfactory economic distribution" of Chesterton's time (and our own). In another place, he speaks of charity being "too much of a manufactured article; and too little of a natural product. The League of Nations is too new to be natural. The modern materialistic humanitarianism is too young to be vigorous."[3] He goes on to say,

"If we want to talk about poverty, we must talk about it as the hunger of a human being, a pain as positive as toothache; and not as the fall in wages or the failure of imports or even the lowering of the economic standard of living . . . we must talk of the human family in language as plain and practical and positive as that in which mystics used to talk of the Holy Family."[4] Christmas recognizes the common humanity of rich and poor alike—for at Christmas, God Himself stooped low enough to be born in squalor. "Christ was obviously conceived as born in a hole in the rocks primarily because it marked the position of one outcast and homeless."[5] In light of God's inexpressible gift (2 Cor. 9:15), Christmas requires that we be liberal in our generosity.

The traditions of Christmas are altogether different from "valuable and honourable traditions of a local and domestic sort." Christmas does not honor the past simply because it is the past, but because it is the truth. The inheritance of faith, as handed down to us, is not a weathered marker in a city cemetery or a faded plaque upon a wall, but a vibrant reality transcending time and place. We honor the past in order to thrive in the present. We conserve the past in order to preserve the future. This is why orthodoxy is no small matter, but of utmost importance. "It is always simple to fall; there are an infinity of angles at which one falls, only one at which one stands," Chesterton tells us. "To have fallen into any one of the fads from Gnosticism to Christian Science would indeed have been obvious and tame. But to have avoided them all has been one whirling adventure; and in my vision the heavenly chariot flies thundering through the ages, the dull heresies sprawling and prostrate, the wild truth reeling but erect."[6] In light of the great cloud of witnesses that has gone before us, Christmas demands that we be conservative in the keeping of "the traditions of our fathers."

If, in the hustle and bustle of the holiday season, we forget to be charitable; if, in the midst of festivity, we forget the past from which the feast came, we have not kept Christmas, but only a pale shadow of it. If, on the other hand, we recognize Christmas for what it really is—a glimpse of a coming kingdom in which righteousness and justice are the foundation of the throne of God (Ps. 89:14)—then we must keep it liberally, we must keep it conservatively, and we must keep it faithfully. Only then may we pray, with all the saints, "Your kingdom come, your will be done, on earth as it is in heaven."

SCRIPTURE READING & REFLECTION

"You shall love the Lord your God with all your heart and with all your soul and with all your mind. This is the great and first commandment. And a second is like it: You shall love your neighbor as yourself."

MATTHEW 22:37-39

How does this passage connect to the ideas explored in today's reading?

What are some ways you can be liberal in your charity and conservative in your keeping of "the traditions of our fathers"?

How is Christmas a picture of the kingdom of heaven?

ON CRACKERS, LOGS, AND THE WINTER BATH OF ECSTASY

The modern world will have to fit in with Christmas or die. Those who will not rejoice in the end of the year must be condemned to lament it. We must accept the New Year as a new fact; we must be born again. No kind of culture or literary experience can save him who entirely refuses this cold bath of winter ecstasy. No poetry can be appreciated by him who cannot appreciate the mottoes in the crackers. No log-rolling can rescue him who will not roll the Yule log. Christmas is like death and child-birth—a test of our simple virtue; and there is no other such test left in this land today.

THE ILLUSTRATED LONDON NEWS (1909)[1]

Perhaps a word of clarification is in order. "The mottoes in the crackers" refers to the English tradition of Christmas crackers—which are not edible crackers, but small packages that pop open when pulled apart, containing a surprise (in Chesterton's day, it was often a motto printed on a small piece of paper). "Rolling the Yule log" most likely refers to a spongy cake rolled into a log-like shape at Christmas—though there is another, more ancient tradition involving a real log burned in a hearth, the sparks and flames of which were rumored to carry prophecies and blessings for the new year.

As you read these words, history is hastening to its inevitable end. One voyage around the sun winds to a close as another begins— one more year in a decade, in a century, in a millennia. As it says in Genesis, "While the earth remains, seedtime and harvest, cold and heat, summer and winter, day and night, shall not cease" (Gen. 8:22). It would behoove us to remember, however, that an ending is also a new beginning, a chance to be born again. "The object of a New Year is not that we should have a new year," Chesterton muses elsewhere. "It is that we should have a new soul and a new nose; new feet, a new backbone, new ears, and new eyes."[2] Reality, as designed by God, testifies to this truth: darkness precedes dawn. Sleep precedes wakefulness. Every morning His mercies are new, as the day is new, as we are new. The land endures the harshness of winter in order to be reborn in the vigor of spring. Everywhere we look, nature is rehearsing resurrection, preparing for the day when *all things* will be made new, when measurable time gives way to immeasurable eternity.

When Chesterton tells us that death, childbirth, and Christmas are tests of simple virtue, what he means is this: how one responds to the miracle of birth, the tragedy of death, and the wonder of the incarnation reveals the "simple virtue" of one's worldview. If new life is not sacred and blessed by the image of God, if death cannot be faced with both dignity and indignation (for death is an impostor), if Christ is not the Savior who came to grant eternal life and overcome the grave, then time will only and always be a curse. It will slip through your fingers. It will entice with illusions of eternal youth, only to steal, kill, and destroy. The author of Ecclesiastes laments that "the race is not to the swift, nor the battle to the strong, nor bread to the wise, nor riches to the intelligent, nor favor to those with knowledge, but time and chance happen to them all" (Eccl. 9:11).

However, if God is in the business to "restore to you the years that the swarming locust has eaten" (Joel 2:25), if "creation itself will be set free from its bondage to corruption" (Rom. 8:21), if "neither death nor life, nor angels nor rulers, nor things present nor things to come, nor powers, nor height nor depth, nor anything else in all cre-ation can separate us from the love of God in Christ" (Rom. 8:35–39), then time itself will be redeemed. As we await the future glory, we can rejoice even as "our outer self is wasting away" (2 Cor. 4:16). We can laugh at the mottoes in the crackers,[3] we can roll the Yule log with cheer—for only those with hope can face the future with con-fident assurance. "Those who will not rejoice in the end of the year must be condemned to lament it."

With gratitude for the year behind us and hopeful expectation for the year ahead, let us be baptized in the "winter bath of ecstasy" and emerge not just with a new year, but with a "new soul, new nose, new feet, new backbone, new ears, new eyes." Let us raise a toast in honor of the God who is the beginning and the end, who holds past and future in His hands, who is the same yesterday, today, and tomorrow, whose kingdom will have no end—for our times are in His hands (Ps. 31:15).

SCRIPTURE READING & REFLECTION

Though our outer self is wasting away, our inner self is being renewed day by day. For this light momentary affliction is preparing for us an eternal weight of glory beyond all comparison, as we look not to the things that are seen but to the things that are unseen. For the things that are seen are transient, but the things that are unseen are eternal.

2 CORINTHIANS 4:17-18

How can you make the most of the time you've been given?

How does the promise of "an eternal weight of glory" affect the way you approach the beginning of a new year?

Try adding some new traditions to your festivities this year. See the Games & Traditions section.

⨞ DAY 30 ⨞

AFTER CHRISTMAS
(AN AFTERWORD)

One of the [strangest] things about our own topsy-turvy
time is that we all hear such a vast amount about Christmas
just before it comes, and suddenly hear nothing at all about it
afterwards. My own trade . . . is trained to begin prophesying
Christmas somewhere about the beginning of autumn: and the
prophecies about it are like prophecies about the Golden Age
and the Day of Judgement combined. Everybody writes about
what a glorious Christmas we are going to have. Nobody, or
next to nobody, ever writes about the Christmas we have just
had. I am going to make myself an exasperating exception in
this matter. I am going to plead for a longer period in which
to find out what was really meant by Christmas; and a fuller
consideration of what we have really found. There are any
number of legends, even of modern legends, about what
happens before Christmas; whether it is the preparation of the
Christmas tree, which is said to date only from the time of the
German husband of Queen Victoria, or the vast population of
Father Christmases who now throng the shops almost as

thickly as the customers. But there is no modern legend of what happens just after Christmas; except a dismal joke about indigestion and the arrival of the doctor.

THE ILLUSTRATED LONDON NEWS (1935)[1]

At the beginning of our travels together, we considered the temptation to celebrate Christmas prematurely. Here, Chesterton laments that Christmas, vastly anticipated and hastily celebrated, is then promptly forgotten, such that we "hear nothing at all about it afterwards." Though it was prophesied with great eloquence, it came and went, and the world moved on to more pressing matters. Granted, if Christmas is nothing more than an excuse for empty revelry, then by all means let it be forgotten as quickly as yesterday's lunch. Let it be a passing mention on the local news. A regional parade. A traveling carnival. A cursory entertainment. If Christmas is treated as such, it is because the modern world does not know what Christmas really is and why it is worth celebrating in the first place.

Chesterton has reminded us, in various ways, of the enduring importance of Christmas. Now he urges us—before moving on to a new year of new concerns, new opportunities, new blessings, new challenges—to consider, earnestly, "the Christmas we have just had." Chesterton speaks of legends about things that happen *before* Christmas—including the numerous traditions we've explored throughout these pages—but notes that there is "no modern legend of what happens after Christmas" (other than "indigestion and the arrival of the doctor"). But perhaps there is a chance that it will not always be so; perhaps there is room to create new legends, new games, new traditions in a world that has largely forgotten such things. May we join him in being an "exasperating exception in this matter"? May we take a moment to meditate on the substance of our traditions, the meaning of our revelries? May we reflect, honestly and earnestly, on "what was really meant by Christmas" and "what we have really found"? Perhaps even those of us who keep Christmas faithfully and reverently will discover that it meant even more than we thought it did, that there was some power at work beneath the surface of our celebrations, shaping and forming us in ways we could scarcely comprehend.

—◦◦◦◦◦—

As Chesterton returns to England from his travels to the East, he finds himself beholding the once-familiar surroundings of London with fresh eyes. He writes:

> I nearly got out of the train at several wayside stations, where I saw secluded cottages which might be brightened by a little news from the Holy Land. For it seemed to me that all my fellow-countrymen must be my friends; all these English places had come much closer together after travels that seemed in comparison as vast as the spaces between the stars. The hop-fields of Kent seemed to me like outlying parts of my own kitchen garden; and London itself to be really situated at London End. London was perhaps the largest of the suburbs of Beaconsfield. By the time I came to Beaconsfield itself, dusk was dropping over the beechwoods and the white cross-roads. The distance seemed to grow deeper and richer with darkness as I went up the long lanes towards my home; and in that distance, as I drew nearer, I heard the barking of a dog.[2]

Perhaps, by the grace of God, Christmas might be known again as a "time when things happen, things which do not always happen." Perhaps, in "traveling backwards through history," we might redis-cover "the place from which Christmas came." Perhaps we might observe with expectant patience the austere season of Advent and then throw ourselves headlong into "a crescendo of festivity until Twelfth Night." Perhaps the paradox of the incarnation will lead us into the presence of the paradoxical God who calls us to Himself. Perhaps the "utter unsuitability of Christmas" will only further our appreciation of it. Perhaps we might encounter "the spirit of liberty" in our familial gatherings, be filled with gratitude for our stockings and the legs that fill them, revel in the uncomfortable comfort of Christmas and allow it to baptize our disenchanted imaginations, to fill us with buoyant hope, and be ushered into the presence of Christ, a "winter fire" in a cold and hostile world.

SCRIPTURE READING & REFLECTION

The true light, which gives light to everyone, was coming into the world. He was in the world, and the world was made through him, yet the world did not know him. He came to his own, and his own people did not receive him. But to all who did receive him, who believed in his name, he gave the right to become children of God, who were born, not of blood nor of the will of the flesh nor of the will of man, but of God.

JOHN 1:9–13

Consider what you have learned over the course of these thirty days. What has God revealed to you?

How has Chesterton encouraged you to see the world with fresh eyes?

Ask Christ, the light of the world, to illuminate your path as you conclude your celebration of Christmas and begin the new year.

POEMS

A CHRISTMAS CAROL

1922[1]

(The Chief Constable has issued a statement declaring that carol singing in the streets by children is illegal, and morally and physically injurious. He appeals to the public to discourage the practice. — Daily Paper.)

God rest you merry gentlemen,
Let nothing you dismay;
The Herald Angels cannot sing,
The cops arrest them on the wing,
And warn them of the docketing
Of anything they say.

God rest you merry gentlemen,
May nothing you dismay:
On your reposeful cities lie
Deep silence, broken only by
The motor horn's melodious cry,
The hooter's happy bray.

So, when the song of children ceased
And Herod was obeyed,
In his high hall Corinthian
With purple and with peacock fan,
Rested that merry gentleman;
And nothing him dismayed.

THE NATIVITY

1897[2]

The thatch on the roof was as golden,
    Though dusty the straw was and old,
The wind had a peal as of trumpets,
    Though blowing and barren and cold,
The mother's hair was a glory
    Though loosened and torn,
For under the eaves in the gloaming
A child was born.

Have a myriad children been quickened.
    Have a myriad children grown old,
Grown gross and unloved and embittered,
    Grown cunning and savage and cold?
God abides in a terrible patience,
    Unangered, unworn,
And again for the child that was squandered
A child is born.

What know we of aeons behind us,
    Dim dynasties lost long ago,
Huge empires, like dreams unremembered,
    Huge cities for ages laid low?
This at least—that with blight and with blessing
    With flower and with thorn,
Love was there, and his cry was among them,
"A child is born."

Though the darkness be noisy with systems,
    Dark fancies that fret and disprove,
Still the plumes stir around us, above us
    The wings of the shadow of love:

Oh! princes and priests, have ye seen it
 Grow pale through your scorn.
Huge dawns sleep before us, deep changes,
A child is born.

And the rafters of toil still are gilded
 With the dawn of the star of the heart,
And the wise men draw near in the twilight,
 Who are weary of learning and art,
And the face of the tyrant is darkened.
 His spirit is torn,
For a new King is enthroned; yea, the sternest,
A child is born.

And the mother still joys for the whispered
 First stir of unspeakable things,
Still feels that high moment unfurling
 Red glory of Gabriel's wings.
Still the babe of an hour is a master
 Whom angels adorn,
Emmanuel, prophet, anointed,
A child is born.

And thou, that art still in thy cradle,
 The sun being crown for thy brow.
Make answer, our flesh, make an answer,
 Say, whence art thou come—who art thou?
Art thou come back on earth for our teaching
 To train or to warn—?
Hush—how may we know?—knowing only
A child is born.

A CHILD OF THE SNOWS

1915[3]

There is heard a hymn when the panes are dim
　　And never before or again,
When the nights are strong with a darkness long,
　　And the dark is alive with rain.

Never we know but in sleet and in snow,
　　The place where the great fires are,
That the midst of the earth is a raging mirth
　　And the heart of the earth a star.

And at night we win to the ancient inn
　　Where the child in the frost is furled,
We follow the feet where all souls meet
　　At the inn at the end of the world.

The gods lie dead where the leaves lie red,
　　For the flame of the sun is flown.
The gods lie cold where the leaves lie gold.
　　And a Child comes forth alone.

A PORTRAIT

Late 1890s[4]

Fair faces crowd on Christmas night
     Like seven suns a-row,
But all beyond is the wolfish wind
     And the crafty feet of the snow.

But through the rout one figure goes
     With quick and quiet tread;
Her robe is plain, her form is frail—
     Wait if she turn her head.

I say no word of line or hue,
     But if that face you see,
Your soul shall know the smile of faith's
     Awful frivolity.

Know that in this grotesque old masque
     Too loud we cannot sing,
Or dance too wild, or speak too wide
     To praise a hidden thing.

That though the jest be old as night,
     Still shaketh sun and sphere
An everlasting laughter
     Too loud for us to hear.

A WORD

Early 1900s[5]

A word came forth in Galilee, a word like to a star;
It climbed and rang and blessed and burnt wherever brave hearts are;
A word of sudden secret hope, of trial and increase
Of wrath and pity fused in fire, and passion kissing peace.
A star that o'er the citied world beckoned, a sword of flame;
A star with myriad thunders tongued: a mighty word there came.

The wedge's dart passed into it, the groan of timber wains,
The ringing of the river nails, the shrieking of the planes;
The hammering on the roofs at morn, the busy workshop roar;
The hiss of shavings drifted deep along the windy floor;
The heat-browned toiler's crooning song, the hum of human worth—
Mingled of all the noise of crafts, the ringing word went forth.

The splash of nets passed into it, the grind of sand and shell,
The boat-hook's clash, the boas-oars' jar, the cries to buy and sell,
The flapping of the landed shoals, the canvas crackling free,
And through all varied notes and cries, the roaring of the sea,
The noise of little lives and brave, of needy lives and high;
In gathering all the throes of earth, the living word went by.

Earth's giants bowed down to it, in Empire's huge eclipse,
When darkness sat above the thrones, seven thunders on her lips,
The woes of cities entered it, the clang of idols' falls,
The scream of filthy Caesars stabbed high in their brazen halls,
The dim hoarse floods of naked men, the world-realms snapping girth,
The trumpets of Apocalypse, the darkness of the earth:

The wrath that brake the eternal lamp and hid the eternal hill,
A world's destruction loading, the word went onward still—
The blaze of creeds passed into it, the hiss of horrid fires,
The headlong spear, the scarlet cross, the hair-shirt and the briars,
The cloistered brethren's thunderous chaunt, the errant
    champion's song,
The shifting of the crowns and thrones, the tangle of the strong.

The shattering fall of crest and crown and shield and cross and cope,
The tearing of the gauds of time, the blight of prince and pope,
The reign of ragged millions leagued to wrench a loaded debt,
Loud with the many-throated roar, the word went forward yet.
The song of wheels passed into it, the roaring and the smoke
The riddle of the want and wage, the fogs that burn and choke.
The breaking of the girths of gold, the needs that creep and swell,
The strengthening hope, the dazing light, the deafening evangel,
Through kingdoms dead and empires damned, through changes
    without cease,
With earthquake, chaos, born and fed, rose,—and the word was
    "Peace."

THE TRUCE OF CHRISTMAS

1904[6]

Passionate peace is in the sky—
And in the snow in silver sealed
The beasts are perfect in the field,
And men seem men so suddenly—
    (But take ten swords and ten times ten
    And blow the bugle in praising men;
    For we are for all men under the sun,
    And they are against us every one;
    And misers haggle and madmen clutch,
    And there is peril in praising much.
    And we have the terrible tongues uncurled
    That praise the world to the sons of the world.)

The idle humble hill and wood
Are bowed upon the sacred birth,
And for one little hour the earth
Is lazy with the love of good—
    (But ready are you, and ready am I,
    If the battle blow and the guns go by;
    For we are for all men under the sun,
    And they are against us every one;
    And the men that hate herd all together,
    To pride and gold, and the great white feather
    And the thing is graven in star and stone
    That the men who love are all alone.)

Hunger is hard and time is tough,
But bless the beggars and kiss the kings,
For hope has broken the heart of things,
And nothing was ever praised enough.
    (But bold the shield for a sudden swing
    And point the sword when you praise a thing,
    For we are for all men under the sun,
    And they are against us every one;
    And mime and merchant, thane and thrall
    Hate us because we love them all;
    Only till Christmastide go by
    Passionate peace is in the sky.)

THE WISE MEN

1913[7]

Step softly, under snow or rain,
    To find the place where men can pray;
The way is all so very plain
That we may lose the way.

Oh, we have learnt to peer and pore
    On tortured puzzles from our youth,
We know all labyrinthine lore,
We are the three wise men of yore,
    And we know all things but the truth.

We have gone round and round the hill
    And lost the wood among the trees,
And learnt long names for every ill,
And served the mad gods, naming still
    The Furies the Eumenides.

The gods of violence took the veil
    Of vision and philosophy,
The Serpent that brought all men bale,
He bites his own accursed tail,
    And calls himself Eternity.

Go humbly . . . it has hailed and snowed . . .
    With voices low and lanterns lit;
So very simple is the road,
    That we may stray from it.

The world grows terrible and white,
    And blinding white the breaking day;
We walk bewildered in the light,
and something is too large for sight,
    And something much too plain to say.

The Child that was ere worlds begun
    (. . . We need but walk a little way,
We need but see a latch undone . . .)
The Child that played with moon and sun
    Is playing with a little hay.

The house from which the heavens are fed,
    The old strange house that is our own,
Where trick of words are never said,
And Mercy is as plain as bread,
    And Honour is as hard as stone.

Go humbly; humble are the skies,
    And low and large and fierce the Star;
So very near the Manger lies
    That we may travel far.

Hark! Laughter like a lion wakes
    To roar to the resounding plain.
And the whole heaven shouts and shakes,
    For God Himself is born again,
And we are little children walking
    Through the snow and rain.

THE HOUSE OF CHRISTMAS

1905–1914[8]

There fared a mother driven forth
Out of an inn to roam;
In the place where she was homeless
All men are at home.
The crazy stable close at hand,
With shaking timber and shifting sand,
Grew a stronger thing to abide and stand
Than the square stones of Rome.

For men are homesick in their homes,
And strangers under the sun,
And they lay their heads in a foreign land
Whenever the day is done.
Here we have battle and blazing eyes,
And chance and honour and high surprise,
Where the yule tale was begun.

A Child in a foul stable,
Where the beasts feed and foam;
Only where He was homeless
Are you and I at home;
We have hands that fashion and heads that know
But our hearts we lost—how long ago!
In a place no chart nor ship can show
Under the sky's dome.

This world is wild as an old wives' tale,
And strange the plain things are,
The earth is enough and the air is enough
For our wonder and our war;
But our rest is as far as the fire-drake swings
And our peace is put in impossible things
Where clashed and thundered unthinkable wings
Round an incredible star.

To an open house in the evening
Home shall men come,
To an older place than Eden
And a taller town than Rome.
To the end of the way of the wandering star,
To the things that cannot be and that are,
To the place where God was homeless
And all men are at home.

A CHRISTMAS CAROL

1896[9]

The Christ-child lay on Mary's lap,
    His hair was like a light.
(O weary, weary were the world,
    But here is all aright.)

The Christ-child lay on Mary's breast,
    His hair was like a star.
(O stem and cunning are the Kings,
    But here the true hearts are.)

The Christ-child lay on Mary's heart,
    His hair was like a fire.
(O weary, weary is the world,
    But here the world's desire.)

The Christ-child stood at Mary's knee,
    His hair was like a crown.
And all the flowers looked up at Him,
    And all the stars looked down.

A LITTLE LITANY

1926[10]

When God turned back eternity and was young,
　　Ancient of Days, grown little for your mirth
(As under the low arch the land is bright)
　　Peered through you, gate of heaven—and saw the earth.

Or shutting out his shining skies awhile
　　Built you about him for a house of gold
To see in pictured walls his storied world
　　Return upon him as a tale is told.

Or found his mirror there; the only glass
　　That would not break with that unbearable light
Till in a corner of the high dark house
　　God looked on God, as ghosts meet in the night.

Star of his morning; that unfallen star
　　In that strange starry overturn of space
When earth and sky changed places for an hour
　　And heaven looked upwards in a human face.

Or young on your strong knees and lifted up
　　Wisdom cried out, whose voice is in the street,
And more than twilight of twiformed cherubim
　　Made of his throne indeed a mercy-seat.

Or risen from play at your pale raiment's hem
　　God, grown adventurous from all time's repose,
Or your tall body climed the ivory tower
　　And kissed upon your mouth the mystic rose.

GLORIA IN PROFUNDIS

ca. 1920[11]

There has fallen on earth for a token
A god too great for the sky.
He has burst out of all things and broken
The bounds of eternity:
Into time and the terminal land
He has strayed like a thief or a lover,
For the wine of the world brims over,
Its splendor is spilt on the sand.

Who is proud when the heavens are humble,
Who mounts if the mountains fall,
If the fixed stars topple and tumble
And a deluge of love drowns all—
Who rears up his head for a crown,
Who holds up his will for a warrant,
Who strives with the starry torrent,
When all that is good goes down?

For in dread of such falling and failing
The fallen angels fell
Inverted in insolence, scaling
The hanging mountain of hell:
But unmeasured of plummet and rod
Too deep for their sight to scan,
Outrushing the fall of man
Is the height of the fall of God.

Glory to God in the Lowest
The spout of the stars in spate—
Where thunderbolt thinks to be slowest
And the lightning fears to be late:
As men dive for sunken gem
Pursuing, we hunt and hound it,
The fallen star has found it
In the cavern of Bethlehem.

hnachten.

ESSAYS

THE SURVIVAL
OF CHRISTMAS

THE ILLUSTRATED LONDON NEWS (1908)[1]

There are two methods of advertisement in the world. One is to advertise something by saying that it is succeeding. The other is to advertise a thing by saying that it is failing. You can advertise ordinary sermons by calling them the New Theology; or on the other hand one can advertise an ordinary flower by asserting (on your personal word of honour) that it is the Last Rose of Summer. The entrance of a thing into the world, or its departure from the world, are the great opportunities for praising it; that is why all healthy men and women have always felt that christenings and funerals were such fun. But in the area of strict advertisement the thing is equally true; you can push a thing by saying that it is coming on; but you can also push a thing by saying that it is going away. To take any two obvious examples: it is an advertisement to say "Positively Largest Circulation" of a newspaper. It is an advertisement also to say "Positively Last Appearance" of an actor. There is, however, a very important distinction between these two methods. If you are going to announce a thing as a failure, it must be a good thing. If you are going to attract attention to the last rose of summer, you must only do it when a long and historical human experience leads you to believe that mankind is really rather fond of roses. You must not play that game with soap, or any slight, faddish, secondary sort of thing.

The sunset is poetical because the sun is popular. Even a slowly fading fire of wood or coal is a thing that can attract people to its last red embers; they will linger over it because real fire is in itself a fine thing. But if you have hot-water pipes in your house (which God forbid), do not, in a light and hospitable manner, ask your friends to come and put their fingers on the hot-water pipes and feel them gradually cooling. It is not the same thing. Fires are nice things, and when half-cold are still poetic; hot-water pipes are nasty things, and the sooner they cool the better. You must be quite certain of the real merit of a thing before you risk a declaration that it is dying. If a thing is weak, insist on its enormous success; it is your only chance. But if a thing is strong, insist that it is defeated.

By this simple principle we can find a really workable division between the two chief types of human institutions. Really healthy institutions are always supposed to be dying—like nations. Thoroughly diseased institutions are always praised as being in a state of brutal and invincible health—like empires. When an Englishman, whether Tory or Radical, wants to praise England he says that England is going to the dogs; that the sturdy English are gone. But when a British Imperialist—whether German, Austrian, Polish, Jewish, or American—wishes to praise the British Empire, he says that it is going ahead like a house on fire, and that nothing can stop its success. He says that because he does not really believe in the British Empire at all; he knows that the optimistic advertisement is the only tip in the case of a shaky piece of goods. But the English patriot, whether Tory or Radical, knows that there is a real sound article called England, and he tells people to snap it up before it has vanished, instead of telling them to buy it merely because it has a boom. This is only one example; but the principle is of universal application. People attached to things they do care about tend to fear for them. People attached to things they do not care about tend to brag about them. Lovers tend to be sad. Commercial travelers tend to be artificially and inhumanly cheerful.

I have been reminded of all this by the inevitable discussions in the current papers about whether the keeping of Christmas is destined to die out, whether Christmas itself will disappear. Of course, Christmas will not disappear. Christmas is one of those very strong things that can afford to boast of its own approaching disappearance. Santa Claus is an actor who can always have a "positively last appearance" with advantage to himself; because people really want him. Weak things must boast of being new, like so many new German philosophies. But strong things can boast of being old. Strong things can boast of being moribund. In the case of Christmas it is quite easy to put a simple test. All the great writers who have praised Christmas customs have praised them as antiquated customs. All the authors who have eulo- gized Father Christmas have eulogized him as a very elderly gentleman.

Now, there is no man who believes in tradition more than I do. Tradition (it seems to me) is simply the democracy of the dead. But there is a certain kind of tradition which, while it is immensely valu- able, is obviously, by reason of its own eternal renewal, not quite accurate. If tradition records that things have been growing more and more hot or cold or blue or triangular, then the longer the tradition has been going on the more clear it must be that it is not quite true. Supposing that your father and grandfather and great-grandfather and great-great-grandfather had all left it on record that the sun in the sky was growing smaller before their very eyes, then I think we should not believe it; not because we are any wiser than they, but because if that had been the exact truth there would not by this time be any sun at all. So that when we find our fathers perpetually saying age after age that religion is dying, that religious festivity is dying, that the hearty human customs are dying, I think we are justified in saying that they were mistaken, not in their praise, but in their despair. The truth was that religion, being really a good thing, could thrive as a continual failure; just as it would be quite worth a brew- er's while to announce the last cask of real ale in England.

The Christmas celebrations will certainly remain, and will certainly survive any attempt by modern artists, idealists, or neo-pagans to substitute anything else for them. For the truth is that there is an alliance between religion and real fun, of which the modern thinkers have never got the key, and which they are quite unable to criticize or to destroy. All Socialist Utopias, all new Pagan Paradises, promised in this age to mankind have all one horrible fault. They are all dignified. All the men in William Morris are dignified. All the men even in H. G. Wells are dignified, when they are men at all. But being undignified is the essence of all real happiness, whether before God or man. Hilarity involves humility; nay, it involves humiliation. Anyone can prove for himself this spiritual principle before a month is out, by walking about in the actual cap that he really found in the cracker. Religion is much nearer to riotous happiness than it is to the detached and temperate types of happiness in which gentlemen and philosophers find their peace. Religion and riot are very near, as the history of all religions proves. Riot means being a rotter; and religion means knowing you are a rotter.

Somebody said, and it has often been quoted: "Be good and you will be happy; but you will not have a jolly time." The epigram is witty, but it is profoundly mistaken in its estimate of the truth of human nature. I should be inclined to say that the truth is exactly the reverse. Be good and you will have a jolly time; but you will not be happy. If you have a good heart you will always have some lightness of heart; you will always have the power of enjoying special human feasts, and positive human good news. But the heart which is there to be lightened will also be there to be hurt; and really if you only want to be happy, to be steadily and stupidly happy like the animals, it may be well worth your while not to have a heart at all. Fortunately, however, being happy is not so important as having a jolly time. Philosophers are happy; saints have a jolly time. The important thing in life is not to keep a steady system of pleasure and composure (which can be done quite well by hardening one's heart or thickening one's head), but to keep alive in oneself the immortal power of astonishment and laughter, and a kind of young reverence. This is why religion always insists on special days like Christmas, while philosophy always tends to despise them. Religion is interested not in whether a man is happy, but whether he is still alive, whether he can still react in a normal way to new things, whether he blinks in a blinding light or laughs when he is tickled. That is the best of Christmas, that it is a startling and disturbing happiness; it is an uncomfortable comfort. The Christmas customs destroy the human habits. And while customs are generally unselfish, habits are nearly always selfish. The object of the religious festival is, as I have said, to find out if a happy man is still alive. A man can smile when he is dead. Composure, resignation, and the most exquisite good manners are, so to speak, the strong points of corpses. There is only one way in which you can test his real vitality, and that is by a special festival. Explode crackers in his ear, and see if he jumps. Prick him with holly, and see if he feels it. If not, he is dead, or, as he would put it, is "living the higher life."

For in this matter, as in nearly all modern matters, we must continually remember the question I think I mentioned recently in connection with Francis Thompson and religious symbolism. When we talk of things like Christmas we must remember what we have to compare them to. It is not a question between Christmas ceremonies and a free, pure life: it is a question between Christmas ceremonies and vulgar society ceremonies; between the exciting conventions of a pantomime and the dull conventions of a dinner-table. It is not Christmas against liberty. Though if it were I should still choose Christmas.

A PROGRESS
FROM ENGLAND

THE ILLUSTRATED LONDON NEWS (1920)[2]

This is written amid fields of snow within a few days of Christmas. And when last I saw snow it was within a few miles of Bethlehem. The coincidence will serve as a symbol of something I have noticed all my life, though it is not very easy to sum up. It is generally the romantic thing that turns out to be the real thing, under the extreme test of realism. It is the skeptical and even rational legend that turns out to be entirely legendary. Everything I had been taught or told led me to regard snow in Bethlehem as a paradox, like snow in Egypt. Every rumor of realism, every indirect form of rationalism, every scientific opinion taken on authority and at third hand, had led me to regard the country where Christ was born solely as a sort of semi-tropical place with nothing but palm-trees and parasols. It was only when I actually looked at it that it looked exactly like a Christmas card. It was only by the sight of my bodily eyes, and against all my mental training, that I realized how true is the tradition headed down in a Christmas carol. The birth and death of Christ, the whole early Christian drama, did not take place on a flat stage called the desert, covered with sand like a circus, and decorated with a few pantomime palm-trees. To begin with, the desert is not flat; and to go on with, the Palestinian hills are not the desert. It might well have been far more like the traditional Christmas scene than any of the learned reconstructions that conceive it as a conventional Oriental scene. The whole background was so mountainous as to be in many ways northern. The shepherds were shepherds of the hills, as certainly as if they had fed their flocks on the Grampian hills like the father of Norval.[3] In truth, Palestine is really a strange and symbolic country; and in nothing more than its series of levels and climates. It is not so much a land as a ladder. Degrees of altitude take the place of degrees of latitude. The Jordan Valley really has the atmosphere of those tropics which seem like the suburbs of hell. But the holy mountain of Jerusalem has really an air of something lifted nearer to heaven. It has the clearness and coldness, not of being nearer to the poles, but of being nearer to the stars.

Now this nameless northern element in the first landscapes of Christianity has had a certain effect on our own history. As the great creed and philosophy which united our fathers swept west' ward over the world, it found its different parts peculiarly fitted to different places. The men of the Mediterranean had, perhaps, a more intimate sense of the meaning of its imagery of the vine. But it succeeded in making its own imagery equally out of the northern holly, and even the heathen mistletoe. And while the Latins more especially preserved the legends about the soldiers, we in the north felt a special link with the legend of the shepherds. We concentrated on Christmas on the element of winter and the wild hills in the old Christian story. Thus Christmas is, in special sense, at once European and English. It is European because it appeals to the reli' gion of Europe. It is English because it specializes in those religious customs that can make even our own landscape a holy land.

The tragedy of England is that she has in these things been grow' ing less English. This would be painfully plain if we could discuss these matters in a detached and dispassionate manner, like an abstract question of art. A recognisable and recognised national character in literature and manners appears long before the end of the Middle Ages. Anybody who recognizes that Dickens is English, as com' pared with Balzac,[4] can also recognise that Chaucer[5] is English, as compared with Boccaccio.[6] As to the moment when that national soul was most supreme and secure of itself, there might be differences of opinion. But no serious observer can doubt that it has since lost its security. The fads that so easily become fashions in our own time would be choked with laughter in their very birth, if that spirit were present in its ancient strength. We recognise an Englishman in Chaucer's Franklin, in whose house "it snowed meat and drink."[7] But he would not recognise an England in which anybody could suggest that it should snow nut cutlets and temperance beverages. He would think he was in a foreign country, not to say another planet.

When we step across the centuries from Chaucer to Dickens, we find the same identical snowstorm raging in the Christmas household of Mr. Wardle at Dingley Dell.[8] And we recognise, in exactly the same way, and neither more nor less, that Mr. Wardle is an Englishman. But though Wardle feels equally secure, Dickens does not feel equally secure. Though the Squire is as comfortable as the Franklin, the modern novelist is not so comfortable as the medieval poet. Dickens is already on the defensive; for he has something to defend. Dickens is not only potentially but positively scornful; for he has something to scorn. The unnatural notions have already begun to eat away the national tradition. The temperance drinks have already appeared though the nut cutlets are not yet. Dickens lived to see people proposing to enforce universal teetotalism, though he did not live, as we or our children may live, to see them bent on enforcing universal vegetarianism. If he had survived to see the proposals which some scientific idealists are already drawing up on paper, it may be that his feelings would have been beyond even his own powers of expression. It may be that the modern world has outstripped satire. I doubt whether even Dickens could have made it funnier than it is.

But the point for the moment is that all this nonsense is in a special sense the loss of a national spirit. Though this progress has largely

ESSAYS

been peculiar to England, it is none the less a progress away from
England. The national movement has been away from the national
idea. It will be noted that nearly all the greatest Englishmen, that
nearly especially the most English Englishmen, were more or less conscious of this. The other great figures between Chaucer and Dickens
are nearly all figures with their faces turned to the past. It is what
makes men call Shakespeare monarchical and medieval; it is what
made Johnson a Tory;[9] it is what made Cobbett so singularly reactionary a Radical.[10] Even the exceptions have exceptional moments
when they are conscious of it: a Puritan like Milton in the rustic
reminiscences of "L'Allegro";[11] a Whig like Addison in the Christmas
ceremonies of Sir Roger de Coverley.[12] Those Christmas ceremonies,
coming down from a time when Chaucer and his Franklin could
enjoy them, have nevertheless suffered all sorts of damage from new
and less liberal philosophies. They were attacked by the Puritans on
theological, by the Utilitarians on economic, and now by the new
Sociologists on hygienic grounds. The new Scrooge wishes to give
everyone else gruel.

A nation may exaggerate itself or fall short of itself; but a nation
must not contradict itself. We should all feel it if the French were to
lose all concern about logic; but there is a real danger of the English
losing all concern about liberty. There is a real danger that the broad
farce and broad freedom which we feel in Chaucer or Dickens will
actually be less apparent among us than among foreign peoples which
have always had more officialism in their law and more classicism
in their literature. The farce is already being thinned by a sort of
tenth-rate idealism bearing the detestable American name of "uplift."
The freedom is already being lost in a network of police prohibition.
Between the Yankee ideality and the Prussian efficiency the English
liberty may well be entirely lost. I should not write this if I did not
think that it may also be saved. But I could not write it without
recording my own conviction that there is only one way of saving it.

We have lost our national instincts because we have lost the idea of that Christendom from which the nations came. In freeing ourselves from Christianity, we have only freed ourselves from freedom. We shall not now return to a merely heathen hilarity, for the new hea-thenism is anything but hilarious. If we do not recover Christmas, we shall never recover Yule.

THE RITUALS
OF CHRISTMAS

THE ILLUSTRATED LONDON NEWS (1927)[13]

hristmas, with its Christmas candles and its hundred shapes and patterns of fire, from the old legend of the log to the blue flames of Snapdragon and the sacred oblation of burning brandy (in the true tradition of sacrifice, which is the destruction of the most precious thing for the glory of the divine powers) has rather irrationally thrown my thoughts back to the flames of a torch-light procession which I saw on the last great ceremonial festival in this city. It was a ritual rather new and national than old and religious. But it was one with which I have a special spiritual sympathy, and about which, at the time, I felt a certain sentiment and formed a certain opinion. I had a reason for not stating the opinion then; and I have a reason for stating the reason now. I could not bring myself to criticize the Armistice celebrations immediately after Armistice Day;[14] because it was just possible that any criticism, which was really critical, might be mistaken for a surrender to that most morbid and unmanly mood of reaction which I have noticed only too often throwing cold water upon those torches which those heroes will carry through history. I would rather join in any mummery, or tolerate any mistakes, than be for one moment mistaken for one of those "modern" persons who have gradually and cautiously, after the peril was over, plucked up courage to preach a religion of cowardice. We have had even poetry prostituted to the service of poltroonery. We have had lyrics loud with panic, of which the best we can say is that their healthiest excuse is shell-shock. But that it is a little difficult to remain charitable when the shocked claims popularity as the shocker. Mean little studies of neurotic paralysis have been put forward as the only realistic record of the one great proof that humanity has given to the heavens of the huge human equality in normal virility and valor. When to this dishonouring of the dead was added the vile indifference and injustice to the living, which has left thousands of the saviours of the world as drifting and desperate as so many old lags out of jail, the reaction to what many would call reason and "normalcy" is not one with which I desire to be connected or confused. And to express anything savouring of disappointment or doubt about the Armistice ceremonies might well have seemed like contributing to that contemptible coldness or striking the same note as did that dreary *diminuendo*. But now, as I say, when we shall soon be in a position to compare such ceremonial with the ancient ceremonials founded by our fathers, in the days when men had an instinct for such things, I think it worth while to remark on some of the memories, and even some of the mistakes, in the more modern formality in its more modern framework. If we are to have ceremonial, Armistice Day has a great deal to learn from Christmas Day, and especially from the days when the Christmas ritual was created.

All ceremony depends on symbol; and all symbols have been vulgarised and made stale by the commercial conditions of our time. This has been especially true since we have felt the commercial infection of America, and progress has turned London, not into a superior London, but into a very inferior New York. Of all these faded and falsified symbols, the most melancholy example is the ancient symbol of the flame. In every civilised age and country, it has been a natural thing to talk of some great festival on which "the town was illuminated." There is no meaning nowadays in saying that the town was illuminated. There is no point or purpose in having it illuminated for any normal and noble enthusiasm, such as the winning of a victory or the granting of a charter. The whole town is illuminated already, but not for noble things. It is illuminated solely to insist on the immense importance of trivial and material things, blazoned from motives entirely mercenary. The significance of such colours and such lights has therefore been entirely killed. It is no good to send up a golden and purple rocket for the glory of the King and Country, or to light a red and raging bonfire on the day of St. George, when everybody is used to seeing the same fiery alphabet proclaiming the importance of Tibble's Tooth Paste or Giggle's Chewing Gum. The new illumination has not, indeed, made Tibble and Giggle so important as St. George and King George; because nothing could. But it has made people weary of the way of proclaiming great things, by perpetually using it to proclaim small things. It has not destroyed the difference between light and darkness, but it has allowed the lesser light to put out the greater.

I was standing in the very heart of this holy town, opposite the Abbey, and within a stone's-throw of the Thames, when I saw the torch-light procession turn the corner and take the road towards the Cenotaph. Now, a torchlight procession is one of the most magnificent of all those instinctive and imaginative institutions by which men have sought to express deep democratic passions of praise or triumph, or lamentation, since the morning of the world. Naturally, by all artistic instinct, they were held at night; and they were held in times and places which were lucky enough to retain a little night. They cannot be done in a garish and feverish civilisation which insists on turning night into day. In those older and simple societies, republics, or kingdoms, there would probably have been enough sense of public authority to command a Curfew, and force all citizens to put out all lights while the pageant of the sacred flames went by. But the modern mind is in an unfathomable muddle about all these things. Our streets are in a permanent dazzle, and our minds in a permanent darkness. It would be an intelligible process to abolish all ceremonies, as the Puritans did. But it is not intelligible to keep ceremonies and spoil them; and nothing in the literature of lunacy is weaker and wilder than the appearance of this wavering sort of lunatic, holding a lighted candle at noon.

A short time ago, the very section of the city in which I was standing was abruptly blotted out by total darkness, the electric light having gone wrong. I wish it had gone wrong at the moment when the marching men turned the corner with all their torches burning. One catastrophe of that sort would have saved the whole situation, and perhaps the whole memory and meaning of the Great War. Its glory would have got a good black background at last; and that moving conflagration would have burned red in men's memories until they died. That was the ceremony as our fathers planned it; and that is also how the ceremonies of Christmas were planned. If we are wise, we shall keep these latter also in the ancient manner, and according to plan. If we must be merely American in our busi-ness, let us at least be civilised in our pleasures. Let us understand, as the artists and the ancient priests and heralds have always under-stood, the meaning of contrast and the conception of a background. If Snapdragon burns with blue flames, do not let us kill it with a white light, with that enterprising spot-light which is so very decid-edly a death-ray. If we have the common-sense to see that red fire-light looks redder in the twilight, let us have the courage to refuse the kind American gentleman's offer of an electric light ten times stronger than day-light. Let us show that the ancient culture, which has produced a picture or two in its time, still knows something about how real pictures are made; even if they are only picture post-cards to be used as Christmas cards.

THE VAST ANTICIPATION
OF CHRISTMAS

THE ILLUSTRATED LONDON NEWS (1933)[15]

ome time in Christmas week, so far as I can calculate, these lines will probably appear in print; thereby violating all the fundamental principles of modern civilisation, defying the normal and necessary laws of Christmas Trade, Christmas Sales, Christmas Numbers, Christmas Shopping, and even a great deal of Christmas greeting; in a word, committing the crime of talking about Christmas quite near to Christmas Day. For the curious custom of our time has turned Christmas into a vast anticipation; by turning it into a vast advertisement. Most journalists have to write their Christmas articles somewhere about the last days of their summer holiday; and prepare to launch them, at the earliest, about the middle of the autumn. They have to stuff their imaginations with holly and mistletoe while gazing at the last rose of summer; or call up a vision of falling snowflakes in a forest of falling leaves. It is a rather peculiar feature of modern times, and is connected with other things that are typically modern. It is perhaps mixed up with that spirit of Prophecy which has made the modern Utopias, and has even led some men to call themselves Futurists, on the quaint supposition that it is possible to be really fond of the future. It is connected with that optimism once romantically expressed in the phrase "a good time coming"; which its simpler supporters might perhaps convey the formula of "now we shan't be long"; which its more sardonic critics might perhaps express in the formula: "jam to-morrow, but never jam to-day." At least, in the matter of the serious prediction of social perfection, it is hardly unfair to say that many would still agree that there is a good time coming, but would find it difficult to agree that now, at this particular moment, we shan't be long. They would still say that Utopia is coming, as some men say that Christmas is coming; especially when they say it (with a shade of bitterness) about the month of March or April. But, under all the official publicity, it is comparatively rare to say that Christmas is coming at the very moment when it really is coming. It is perhaps even rarer to say, with a solid and complete satisfaction, that Christ has come.

For the Futurist fashion of our time has led nearly everybody to look for happiness to-morrow rather than to-day. Thus, while there is an incessant and perhaps even increasing fuss about the approach of the festivities of Christmas, there is rather less fuss than there ought to be about really making Christmas festive. Modern men have a vague feeling that when they have come to the feast, they have come to the finish. By modern commercial customs, the preparations for it have been so very long and the practice of it seems so very short. This is, of course, in sharp contrast to the older traditional customs, in the days when it was a sacred festival for a simpler people. Then the preparation took the form of the more austere season of Advent and the fast of Christmas Eve. But when men passed on to the feast of Christmas it went on for a long time after the feast of Christmas Day. It always went on for a continuous holiday of rejoicing for at least twelve days, and only ended in that wild culmination which Shakespeare described as "Twelfth Night: or What You Will." That is to say, it was a sort of Saturnalia which ended in anybody doing whatever he would; and in William Shakespeare writing some very beautiful and rather irrelevant poetry round a perfectly impossible story about a brother and sister who looked exactly alike. In our more enlightened times, the perfectly impossible stories are printed in magazines a month or two before Christmas has begun at all; and in the hustle and hurry of this early publication, the beautiful poetry is, somehow or other, left out.

It were vain to conceal my own reactionary prejudice; which deludes me into thinking there is something to be said for the older manner. I am so daring as darkly to suspect that it would be better if people could enjoy Christmas when it came, instead of being bored with the news that it was coming. I even think it might be better to be the naughty little boy who falls sick through eating too much Christmas pudding, than to be the more negative and nihilistic little boy who is sick of seeing pictures of Christmas pudding in popular periodicals or coloured hoardings, for months before he gets any pudding at all.

At any rate, the proof of the Christmas pudding is in the eating. And it stands as a symbol of a whole series of things, which too many people nowadays have forgotten how to enjoy in themselves, and for themselves, and at the time when they are actually consumed. Far too much space is taken up with the names of things rather than the things themselves; with designs and plans and pictorial announcements of certain objects, rather than with the real objects when they are really objective. The world we know is far too full of rumors and reports and reflected reputations, instead of the direct appreciation by appetite and actual experience. The difficulty always presented to those who would restore men to a simpler life on the land, for instance, is always some form of the objection (true or false) that modern men would be dull if they dealt with real land on a farm, instead of unreal landscape in a film. As a fact, the farm landscape has a hundred interesting things in it which the film landscape has not. But the critics cannot bring themselves to believe that a man will ever again have a taste for going back to the originals, as more interesting than the copies. For all the apparent materialism and mass mechanism of our present culture, we, far more than any of our fathers, live in a world of shadows. It is none the less so because the prophets and progressives tell us eagerly that these are coming events which cast their shadow before. It is assumed that nothing is really thrilling except a dance of shadows; and we miss the very meaning of substance.

There is another way in which the Christmas pudding, though substantial enough, is itself an allegory and a sign. The little boy expects to find sixpences in the pudding; and this is right enough, so long as the sixpences are secondary to the pudding. Now the change from the medieval to the modern world might be very truly described under that image. It is all the difference between putting sixpences in a Christmas pudding and erecting a Christmas pudding round sixpences. There was money in the old days of Christmas and Christendom; there was merchandise; there were merchants. But the moral scheme of all the old order, whatever its other vices and dis-eases, always assumed that money was secondary to substance: that the merchant was secondary to the maker. Windfalls of money came to this man and that, as shillings and sixpences are extracted excitedly from Christmas puddings. But the idea of normal owning or enjoy-ing preponderated over the idea of accidental or adventurous gain. With the rise of the merchant adventurers the whole world gradu-ally changed, until the preponderance was all the other way. The world was dominated by what the late Lord Birkenhead described as "the glittering prizes," without which, as he appeared to believe, men could not be really moved to any healthy or humane activity. And it is true that men came to think too much about prizes, and too little about pudding. This, in connection with ordinary pudding, is a fallacy: in connection with Christmas pudding it is a blasphemy. For there is truly something of perversity, not unmixed with pro-fanity, about the notion of trade completely transforming a tradi-tion of such sacred origin. Millions of perfectly healthy and worthy men and women still keep Christmas; and do in all sincerity keep it holy as well as happy. But there are some, profiting by such natural schemes of play and pleasure-seeking, who have used it for things far baser than either pleasure-seeking or play. They have betrayed Christmas. For them the substance of Christmas, like the substance of Christmas pudding, has become stale stuff in which their own treasure is buried; and they have only multiplied the sixpences into thirty pieces of silver.

THE WINTER FEAST

G.K.'S WEEKLY (1936)[16]

I t is the greatest glory of the Christian tradition that it has incorporated so many Pagan traditions. But it is most glorious of all, to
my mind, when they are popular traditions. And the best and most
obvious example is the way in which Christianity did incorporate, in
so far as it did incorporate, the old human and heathen conception of
the Winter Feast . . .

There is a perfectly natural parallel between a religion that defies
the world and a ritual that defies the weather. Heathenism in the
sense of hedonism, the concentration of the mind on pure pleasure
as such, would chiefly concentrate on the conception of a Summer
Feast. But in winter even a rich man receives some faint hint of the
problem of a poor man; he may avoid being hungry, but he cannot
always avoid being cold. To choose that moment of common freezing
for the assertion of common fraternity is, in its own intrinsic nature, a
foreshadowing of what we call the Christian idea. It involves the suggestion that joy comes from within and not from without. It involves
the suggestion that peril and the potentiality of pain are themselves
a ground for gratitude and rejoicing. It involves the suggestion that
even when we are merely Pagans, we are not merely Pantheists.
We are not merely Nature-worshippers; because Man smiles when
Nature frowns. It has always involved, under varying limitations in
varying societies, the idea of hospitality, especially hospitality to the
stranger and generally to the poor. Of course there are perfectly natural reasons for wanting to drink wine or warm ourselves at the fire

in winter; but that is not an answer, except to those who have the ill-informed prejudice that Christianity must be opposed to things merely because they are natural. The point is in making a point of it; the special interest is in the special occasion, in the fact that during the Winter Feast, whether Pagan or Christian, there always was in some degree the idea of extending the enjoyment to others, of passing round the wine or seating the wanderer by the hearth. It is no con-troversial point against the Christians that they felt they could take up and continue such traditions among the Pagans; it only shows that the Christians knew a Christian thing when they saw it. . . .

This real history of Christmas is very relevant to the real crisis of Christendom. We live in a terrible time of war and rumor of war; with a barbaric danger of the real reaction that goes back, not to the old form, but to the old formlessness. International idealism in its effort to hold the world together in a peace that can resist wars and revolutions, is admittedly weakened and often disappointed. I should say simply that it does not go deep enough. Christianity could draw life out of the depths of Paganism; but mere Modernism cannot draw on the depths of either. Charity is too much of a manufactured article and too little of a natural product. The League of Nations is too new to be natural. The modern materialistic humanitarianism is too young to be vigorous. If we really wish to make vivid the hor-rors of destruction and mere disciplined murder, we must see them more simply as attacks on the hearth and the human family; and feel about Hitler as men felt about Herod. If we want to talk about pov-erty, we must talk about it as the hunger of a human being, a pain as positive as toothache; and not as the fall in wages or the failure of imports or even the lowering of the economic standard of living. We must say first of the beggar, not that there is insufficient housing accommodation but that he has nowhere to lay his head. We must say first of the human family, not that there are no jobs for them in the factory, but that there is no room for them in the inn. That is, we must talk of the human family in language as plain and practical and positive as that in which mystics used to talk of the Holy Family. We must learn again to use the naked words that describe a natural thing; and dispense for a moment with all those sociological poly-syllables, with which an artificial society has learned to talk of it as an artificial thing. Then we shall draw on the driving force of many thousand years; and call up a real humanitarianism out of the depths of humanity.

With Every Good Wish for Christmas.

ESSAYS

SHORT STORIES

THE SHOP OF GHOSTS

1909[1]

Nearly all the best and most precious things in the universe you can get for a halfpenny. I make an exception, of course, of the sun, the moon, the earth, people, stars, thunderstorms, and such trifles. You can get them for nothing. Also I make an exception of another thing, which I am not allowed to mention in this paper, and of which the lowest price is a penny halfpenny. But the general principle will be at once apparent. In the street behind me, for instance, you can now get a ride on an electric tram for a halfpenny. To be on an electric tram is to be on a flying castle in a fairy tale. You can get quite a large number of brightly coloured sweets for a halfpenny. Also you can get the chance of reading this article for a halfpenny; along, of course, with other and irrelevant matter.

But if you want to see what a vast and bewildering array of valuable things you can get at a halfpenny each you should do as I was doing last night. I was gluing my nose against the glass of a very small and dimly lit toy shop in one of the greyest and leanest of the streets of Battersea. But dim as was that square of light, it was filled (as a child once said to me) with all the colours God ever made. Those toys of the poor were like the children who buy them; they were all dirty; but they were all bright. For my part, I think brightness more important than cleanliness; since the first is of the soul, and the second of the body. You must excuse me; I am a democrat;[2] I know I am out of fashion in the modern world.

As I looked at that palace of pigmy wonders, at small green

omnibuses, at small blue elephants, at small black dolls, and small red
Noah's arks, I must have fallen into some sort of unnatural trance.
That lit shop-window became like the brilliantly lit stage when one
is watching some highly coloured comedy. I forgot the grey houses
and the grimy people behind me as one forgets the dark galleries and
the dim crowds at a theatre. It seemed as if the little objects behind
the glass were small, not because they were toys, but because they
were objects far away. The green omnibus was really a green omnibus, a green Bayswater omnibus, passing across some huge desert on
its ordinary way to Bayswater. The blue elephant was no longer blue
with paint; he was blue with distance. The black doll was really a
[native] relieved against passionate tropic foliage in the land where
every weed is flaming and only man is black. The red Noah's ark was
really the enormous ship of earthly salvation riding on the rain-swol-
len sea, red in the first morning of hope.

Every one, I suppose, knows such stunning instants of abstraction, such brilliant blanks in the mind. In such moments one can see
the face of one's own best friend as an unmeaning pattern of specta-
cles or mustaches. They are commonly marked by the two signs of
the slowness of their growth and the suddenness of their termina-
tion. The return to real thinking is often as abrupt as bumping into a
man. Very often indeed (in my case) it is bumping into a man. But in
any case the awakening is always emphatic and, generally speaking, it
is always complete. Now, in this case, I did come back with a shock
of sanity to the consciousness that I was, after all, only staring into
a dingy little toy-shop; but in some strange way the mental cure did
not seem to be final. There was still in my mind an unmanageable
something that told me that I had strayed into some odd atmosphere,
or that I had already done some odd thing. I felt as if I had worked
a miracle or committed a sin. It was as if I had at any rate, stepped
across some border in the soul.

To shake off this dangerous and dreamy sense I went into the shop and tried to buy wooden soldiers. The man in the shop was very old and broken, with confused white hair covering his head and half his face, hair so startlingly white that it looked almost artificial. Yet though he was senile and even sick, there was nothing of suffering in his eyes; he looked rather as if he were gradually falling asleep in a not unkindly decay. He gave me the wooden soldiers, but when I put down the money he did not at first seem to see it; then he blinked at it feebly, and then he pushed it feebly away.

"No, no," he said vaguely. "I never have. I never have. We are rather old-fashioned here."

"Not taking money," I replied, "seems to me more like an uncommonly new fashion than an old one."

"I never have," said the old man, blinking and blowing his nose; "I've always given presents. I'm too old to stop."

"Good heavens!" I said. "What can you mean? Why, you might be Father Christmas."

"I am Father Christmas," he said apologetically, and blew his nose again.

The lamps could not have been lighted yet in the street outside. At any rate, I could see nothing against the darkness but the shining shop-window. There were no sounds of steps or voices in the street; I might have strayed into some new and sunless world. But something had cut the chords of common sense, and I could not feel even surprise except sleepily. Something made me say, "You look ill, Father Christmas."

"I am dying," he said.

I did not speak, and it was he who spoke again.

"All the new people have left my shop. I cannot understand it. They seem to object to me on such curious and inconsistent sort of grounds, these scientific men, and these innovators. They say that I give people superstitions and make them too visionary; they say I give people sausages and make them too coarse. They say my heavenly parts are too heavenly; they say my earthly parts are too earthly; I don't know what they want, I'm sure. How can heavenly things be too heavenly, or earthly things too earthly? How can one be too good, or too jolly? I don't understand. But I understand one thing well enough. These modern people are living and I am dead."

"You may be dead," I replied. "You ought to know. But as for what they are doing, do not call it living."

A silence fell suddenly between us which I somehow expected to be unbroken. But it had not fallen for more than a few seconds when, in the utter stillness, I distinctly heard a very rapid step coming nearer and nearer along the street. The next moment a figure flung itself into the shop and stood framed in the doorway. He wore a large white hat tilted back as if in impatience; he had tight black old-fashioned pantaloons, a gaudy old-fashioned stock and waistcoat, and an old fantastic coat. He had large, wide-open, luminous eyes like those of an arresting actor; he had a pale, nervous face, and a fringe of beard. He took in the shop and the old man in a look that seemed literally a flash and uttered the exclamation of a man utterly staggered.

"Good lord!" he cried out; "it can't be you! It isn't you! I came to ask where your grave was."

"I'm not dead yet, Mr. Dickens," said the old gentleman, with a feeble smile; "but I'm dying," he hastened to add reassuringly.

"But, dash it all, you were dying in my time," said Mr. Charles Dickens with animation; "and you don't look a day older."

"I've felt like this for a long time," said Father Christmas.

Mr. Dickens turned his back and put his head out of the door into the darkness.

"Dick," he roared at the top of his voice; "he's still alive."

Another shadow darkened the doorway, and a much larger and more full-blooded gentleman in an enormous periwig came in, fanning his flushed face with a military hat of the cut of Queen Anne. He carried his head well back like a soldier, and his hot face had even a look of arrogance, which was suddenly contradicted by his eyes, which were literally as humble as a dog's. His sword made a great clatter, as if the shop were too small for it.

"Indeed," said Sir Richard Steele,[3] "'tis a most prodigious matter, for the man was dying when I wrote about Sir Roger de Coverley[4] and his Christmas Day."

My senses were growing dimmer and the room darker. It seemed to be filled with newcomers.

"It hath ever been understood," said a burly man, who carried his head humorously and obstinately a little on one side (I think he was Ben Jonson)[5] "It hath ever been understood, consule Jacobo, under our King James and her late Majesty, that such good and hearty customs were fallen sick, and like to pass from the world. This grey beard most surely was no lustier when I knew him than now."

And I also thought I heard a green-clad man, like Robin Hood, say in some mixed Norman French, "But I saw the man dying."

"I have felt like this a long time," said Father Christmas, in his feeble way again.

Mr. Charles Dickens suddenly leant across to him.

"Since when?" he asked. "Since you were born?"

"Yes," said the old man, and sank shaking into a chair. "I have been always dying."

Mr. Dickens took off his hat with a flourish like a man calling a mob to rise.

"I understand it now," he cried, "you will never die."

THE NEW CHRISTMAS

1926[6]

As the Three Wise Men brought gifts to Bethlehem, so did the Three Wiser Men of that wiser world of which the new prophets tell us bring gifts to that city which is brighter than Bethlehem, which is or will be a perfect blend of Boston and Babylon and Birmingham, but perfecting the perfections of all three. The First King, who had once been known as the Radium[7] King, had later risen to the title of the Aetherite King, being named after that great new metal so much more precious than gold and so much more sharp and piercing than steel. In that empire of knowledge and power, a precious metal was not merely dug up as a dog digs up a bone; but by scientific analysis and combination precipitated out of the void like frozen lightning; as if born within the mind of man. Nor was it childishly hoarded like gold in a casket, but wrought into a hundred shining shapes to delight and serve the child of all the ages; wheels of blinding speed or engines whose stature reached the stars; all the towering things that can be made by man were brought as toys before the child. And the Second King was the lord not of incense only, but of all the graduated odours of the great new science of scent; whereby men could manufacture the atmosphere about them and almost create a climate like men creating a sky. Clouds like the clouds of the morning and evening hung above their march like banners and all the scents of Asia passed through them like changing tunes. But these also were far removed from their rudimentary natural elements and being rarified by analysis had also something of the abstraction of music. And although the Third King in some sense continued with a faint tradition of burial and the bitterness of myrrh, the same adaptation had brought these things far beyond such rude and remote beginnings; for there went with him the chemical fires of crematoria and a lulling breath of lethal chambers; and his disinfectants were the most delightful in the world.

As the moving marble causeway across the desert bore the motionless groups nearer to their destination, they talked a little of the wide range of gifts, and how they had been planned to express all the achievements of humanity; and hoped that nothing was lacking to the completeness.

"There is no reason why anything whatever should be lacking," said the First King a little sharply. "Now that our processes are perfected, there is nothing that cannot be done. We have only to perceive a lack and supply it."

"The only danger is," replied the Second King, "that in such fulness we should not perceive anything lacking. Even in your vast and marvellous machinery some tiny screw may be loose."

"It is strange that you should say so," said the Last King, in his more funereal voice. "I cannot get rid of a foolish sense that I may have lost some little thing or left it behind."

And when they had come to the New Bethlehem, curiously enough, they noticed that the official in charge of the operations, an eminent electrical engineer whose name was Joseph, was walking rapidly to and fro with something of a worried or at least a puzzled look. He also had something of the air of trying to remember what he had forgotten. Presently the advance halted; and in front of them there seemed to be some fumbling of delay.

"I thought there was a hitch somewhere," said the Second King, frowning: "Now that we have learnt to leave nothing to nature, it is exasperating to be checked by some complication in our own arrangements. I shall make searching inquiries at once."

He stepped forward and conferred briefly with the frowning Joseph; then he turned to them again, his own face wearing a frown. He scowled a moment at all the forest of gigantic gifts and then said curtly:

"I knew there was some mistake. They have neglected to procure a child."

RECIPES

TURKEY[1]

INGREDIENTS

- Turkey (whole)
- Melted butter
- Bacon strips or salt pork (if desired)
- Baste (either melted fat, fruit juice, white wine, or pan drippings)
- Seasoning (onion, garlic, thyme, rosemary, sage)

INSTRUCTIONS

Roasting

Place turkey, breast side up, on a rack in an uncovered pan.

Brush the turkey with melted fat, and cover with a light cloth dipped in melted, unsalted fat.

Cover the breast, legs, and wings well.

If desired, strips of bacon or salt pork can be placed at intervals along the breast, legs, and wings, then covered with a light, clean cloth.

Roast at 325°F, until tender. 25 minutes per pound for birds under 12 pounds, or 20 minutes per pound for larger birds.

Baste turkey several times, either with melted fat, fruit juice, white wine, or pan drippings throughout roasting.

Season turkey with herbs halfway through roasting.

Remove the cloth for the last 45 minutes, so that the turkey will be sufficiently browned.

Carving

Place large fork into the turkey, straddling the breast bone. Cut through the skin around the thigh, then press blade back, so that ligaments may be easily cut. Set aside. Repeat with wings, set aside also.

Still with the fork in breast bone, slice white meat from breast, thinly.

After slicing white meat, cut up legs and wings. Insert fork in leg, holding it parallel to drumstick. Separate drumstick from thigh by cutting through exposed joint. Thigh, if large, may be used for 2 or 3 portions. Each serving should have both white and dark meat, placed over a spoonful of dressing.

TO DRESS TURKEY WITH RED BUTTONS (Optional): Stick a toothpick through a red cranberry and place about 1 inch apart from breast bone to neck. A stick of celery curled at both ends makes a bow tie.

GIBLET GRAVY[2]

INGREDIENTS

- Turkey drippings
- Flour
- Cold water
- Salt
- Pepper
- Chopped, cooked giblets

INSTRUCTIONS

As soon as it is done, remove turkey to a hot platter, and keep it hot.

Turn the fat out of the roasting pan, into a pan on the stove. Measure out 2 tablespoons of it for every cupful of gravy you wish to make.

Now add the same amount of flour as you have fat, stirring constantly over low heat.

Cook gently until golden brown.

Add cold water: 1 cup for every 2 tablespoons of fat used.

Stir until gravy is smooth and thickened.

Add salt, pepper, and cooked giblets to taste.

A TURKEY REVERIE

THE ILLUSTRATED LONDON NEWS, 1906[3]

I do not know whether an animal killed at Christmas has had a better or a worse time than it would have had if there had been no Christmas or no Christmas dinners. But I do know that the fighting and suffering brotherhood to which I belong and owe everything, Mankind, would have a much worse time if there were no such thing as Christmas or Christmas dinners. Whether the turkey which Scrooge gave to Bob Cratchit had experienced a lovelier or more melancholy career than that of less attractive turkeys is a subject upon which I cannot even conjecture. But that Scrooge was better for giving the turkey and Cratchit happier for getting it I know as two facts, as I know that I have two feet. What life and death may be to turkey is not my business; but the soul of Scrooge and the body of Cratchit are my business. Nothing shall induce me to darken human homes, to destroy human festivities, to insult human gifts and human benefactions for the sake of some hypothetical knowledge which Nature curtained from our eyes. We men and women are all in the same boat, upon a stormy sea. We owe to each other a terrible and tragic loyalty. If we catch sharks for food, let them be killed most mercifully; let any one who likes love the sharks, and pet the sharks, and tie ribbons round their necks and give them sugar and teach them to dance. But if once a man suggests that a shark is to be valued against a sailor, or that the poor shark might be permitted to bite off a [native]'s leg occasionally; then I would court-martial the man—he is a traitor to the ship.

Meanwhile, it remains true that I shall eat a great deal of turkey this Christmas; and it is not in the least true (as the vegetarians say) that shall do it because I do not realize what I am doing, or because I do what I know is wrong, or that I do it with shame or doubt or a fundamental unrest of conscience. In one sense I know quite well what I am doing; in another sense I know quite well that I know not what I do. Scrooge and the Cratchits and I are, as I have said, all in one boat; the turkey and I are, to say the most of it, ships that pass in the night, and greet each other in passing. I wish him well; but it is really practically impossible to discover whether I treat him well. I can avoid, and I do avoid with horror, all special and artificial tormenting of him, sticking pins in him for fun or sticking knives in him for scientific investigation. But whether by feeding him slowly and killing him quickly for the needs of my brethren, I have improved in his own solemn eyes his own strange and separate destiny, whether I have made him in the sight of God slave or a martyr, or one whom the gods love and who die young—that is far more removed from my possibilities of knowledge than the most abstruse intricacies of mysticism or theology. A turkey is more occult and awful than all the angels and archangels. In so far as God has partly revealed to us an angelic world, he has partly told us what an angel means. But God has never told us what a turkey means. And if you go and stare at a live turkey for an hour or two, you will find by the end of it that the enigma has rather increased than diminished.

SAUSAGE ROLLS

INGREDIENTS

- 14 ounces all-butter puff pastry
- 1 pound sausage meat
- 1 medium onion, grated
- 4 tablespoons of chopped sage leaves (or dried)
- 1 egg, beaten

INSTRUCTIONS

Preheat oven to 425°F.

In a large bowl, mix the sausage meat, onion, and sage together and set aside.

Remove the pastry from the fridge and roll out on a floured surface into an oblong shape measuring 15"x12". Cut this into three long strips and divide the sausage meat into three, making three long rolls the same length as the pastry.

The sausage meat may be sticky, so use a little flour in your hands to make it easier to handle, if needed.

Take a spoonful of sausage meat and place onto each of the pastry strips, then fold over and seal along the edge. The sausage meat might be sticky.

Cut into individual rolls approximately 3" long. Snip two slits on the top of each roll to allow the steam to escape.

Brush with beaten egg.

Place the sausage rolls onto the baking sheet and bake for 20–25 minutes until golden brown, then place on a wire rack to cool.

WASSAIL

INGREDIENTS

- 2 apples
- 8 cups apple cider
- 2 cups orange juice
- 1/3 cup lemon juice
- 4 cinnamon sticks
- 15 whole cloves
- 1/4 teaspoon ground ginger
- 1/4 teaspoon ground nutmeg
- 1 tablespoon light brown sugar

INSTRUCTIONS

Insert cloves into apples.

Add all ingredients to large pot over low-medium heat.

Bring to simmer. Simmer for 30–45 minutes.

Remove apples and cloves. Serve in mugs.

MINCE PIES

INGREDIENTS

- 20 ounces sweet mincemeat conserve
- 12 ounces plain flour
- A pinch of salt
- 3 ounces lard
- 3 ounces butter
- Milk
- Powdered sugar
- Small aluminum pie tins
- Circular or fluted 3" pastry cutter
- Circular or fluted 2.5" pastry cutter

INSTRUCTIONS

Preheat oven to 425°F.

Sift the flour into the mixing bowl with a little salt. Add the lard and rub gently until the mixture resembles breadcrumbs. Then add a little water until the mixture comes together and leaves the bowl clean.

Leave the pastry to rest in the fridge for 30 minutes covered with cling film to prevent it drying out.

Divide the mixture into two and roll out both as thinly as possible. Cut out the larger size rounds from one and the smaller size from the other half. Any excess pastry can be gathered up and rolled again.

Lightly grease the pie tin and line with the larger pastry rounds.

Fill with mincemeat and place the smaller pastry round on top to form a lid sealing the edges.

Brush each one with milk. Snip a slit in the top to allow steam to escape and place in the oven for around 25 minutes until golden brown.

Remove and cool on a wire rack.

When cool, sieve the powdered sugar over them to decorate. The pies can be stored in a tin until required.

BRANDY BUTTER

INGREDIENTS

- 6 ounces unsalted butter at room temperature
- 6 ounces soft dark brown sugar
- 6 tablespoons of brandy (or dark rum)

INSTRUCTIONS

Place the butter and sugar into a bowl and blend together using an electric hand whisk until it is pale and creamy. Or, if you prefer, this can be done in a food processor.

Slowly add the brandy or rum a little at a time, beating the mixture as you go.

Place the butter into a small bowl or container and place in the fridge until needed.

The butter will keep well in the fridge for up to three weeks.

A tasty addition to mince pies!

FRUIT CRUMBLE

INGREDIENTS

- 1 large can of sliced peaches, drained (or any fruit, such as apples, peaches, blackberries, or rhubarb)
- 2.5 cups flour
- 2 sticks butter
- 3/4 cup brown raw sugar (raw cane sugar)
- A pinch of cinnamon powder

INSTRUCTIONS

Preheat oven to 375°F.

In a large bowl add the flour, cinnamon, and butter (cut up the butter into small pieces to make it easier for mixing).

Rub the mixture together until it resembles fine breadcrumbs. This part takes a while. If it's still too wet, add a little more flour. If too dry, add more butter.

Stir in the sugar.

Sprinkle all the mixture over the peaches in a medium-sized casserole dish.

Bake for 25 minutes or until crisp and brown on top.

Serve hot with evaporated milk or ice cream.

HARD SAUCE[4]

INGREDIENTS

- 1/3 cup butter, room temperature
- 1 cup powdered sugar
- 3/4 teaspoon vanilla
- 1/2 teaspoon brandy flavoring
- 1 tablespoon cream

INSTRUCTIONS

Beat cream and butter together until well mixed. Cream butter.

Beat in sugar gradually and continue creaming until fluffy.

Add vanilla and brandy flavoring.

Drizzle over Christmas pudding.

CHRISTMAS PUDDING[5]

INGREDIENTS

- 1 small cooking apple peeled and chopped
- 1 cup raisins
- 1/2 cup golden raisins
- 1/2 cup chopped prunes
- 1/2 cup dried currants
- Zest of 1 lemon
- Zest of 1 orange
- 3/4 cup bourbon or brandy, more if needed
- 1/2 cup unsalted butter
- 1 cup brown sugar
- 2 tablespoons molasses
- 2 eggs
- 1 cup breadcrumbs
- 1/2 cup all-purpose flour
- 1/4 cup coarsely chopped almonds
- 1/2 teaspoon baking powder
- 1/4 teaspoon kosher salt
- 1 teaspoon ground cinnamon
- 1/4 teaspoon ground nutmeg
- 1/4 teaspoon ground cloves

INSTRUCTIONS

Combine all fruits and zest in a bowl and soak in bourbon or brandy overnight, covered.

Beat together butter, molasses, and brown sugar until creamy. Add eggs and beat again until fluffy. Add fruit mixture and fold in.

In a large mixing bowl combine flour, salt, almonds, baking powder, bread crumbs, and all spices together.

Add the flour mixture to the liquid and fruit mixture. Final mixture may seem moist, but do not add flour.

Grease a large pudding tin that will fit inside of a large Dutch oven or tall pot to create a double boiler.

Fill pudding tin with batter and cover tightly with aluminum foil.

Place a small glass bowl or ramekin at the bottom of the Dutch oven. Place covered pudding tin on top of ramekin and carefully fill Dutch oven with water until it is halfway up the side of the pudding tin.

Bring to a boil and reduce heat to simmer. Place a lid on top of the Dutch oven and let steam for 5 hours. Add water as needed.

Carefully remove from water and let cool completely.

Garnish with powdered sugar and a holly berry sprig.

A WORD ON THE
WHOLESOMENESS OF
CHRISTMAS PUDDING

THE ILLUSTRATED LONDON NEWS, 1906[6]

Christmas and hygiene are commonly in some antagonism, and I, for one, am heartily on the side of Christmas. Glancing down a newspaper column I see the following alarming sentence: "The Lancet adds a frightful corollary that the only way to eat Christmas pudding with perfect impunity is to eat it alone." At first the mean-ing of this sentence deceived me. I thought it meant that the eater of Christmas pudding must be in a state of sacred isolation like an anchorite at prayer. I thought it meant that the presence of one's fellow creatures in some way disturbed the subtle nervous and diges-tive process through which Christmas pudding was beneficent. It sounded rather mad and wicked, certainly; but not madder or more wicked than many other things that I have read in scientific journals.

But on re-reading the passage, I see that my first impression did the Lancet an injustice. The sentence really means that when one eats Christmas pudding one should eat nothing but Christmas pud-ding. "It is," says the Lancet, "a complete meal in itself." This is, I should say, a question of natural capacity, not to say of cubic capac-ity. I know a kind of person who would find one Christmas pudding a complete meal in itself, and even a little over.

For my own part, I should say that three, or perhaps four, Christmas puddings might be said to constitute a complete meal in themselves. But, in any case, this sudden conversion of science to plum-pudding is a fine example of the fickleness of the human intellect and the steadiness of the human appetite. Scientific theories change, but the plum-pudding remains the same, century after century (I do not mean the individual pudding, but the type), a permanent monument of human mysticism and human mirth. If there is one thing more than another which from our childhood we have heard was grossly unwholesome and opposed to all medical advice, that thing certainly was Christmas pudding. Now it seems (again by the best medical advice) that to call Christmas pudding wholesome is entirely a faint and approximate expression of its merits. Not only is Christmas pudding wholesome, but it is so peculiarly and incomparably wholesome that no other and less medical substance must be taken with it so as to spoil its perfect medical effect.

GAMES & TRADITIONS

CHRISTMAS CRACKERS

The popular British tradition of Christmas crackers originated in the mid-1800s with the confectioner Tom Smith, who had discovered the French *bonbon* (a chocolate nestled in a twisted wrapper) and brought it back to England. When sales of the Anglo-fied *bonbons* suffered, he decided to include a message in the wrapper, along with a snapping mechanism. When the two ends of the package were pulled, it would pop open, revealing the treat (and the message) inside. Today, Christmas crackers remain a popular tradition in England (and other countries), but the messages have largely been replaced with small toys and trinkets.

SIXPENCE IN PUDDING

As earlier established, the tradition of hiding sixpence in Christmas pudding traces back to the time of Queen Victoria and her husband Prince Albert. A week before Advent, a silver sixpence coin would be hidden in the Christmas pudding that was being prepared in advance for Christmas Day. When eaten, whoever found the sixpence would be blessed with luck and good fortune for the following year.

For a Christmas pudding recipe, refer to the Recipes section.

WASSAILING

Wassailing—from the Anglo-Saxon *waes hael* ("good health")— is a time-honored tradition involving the communal imbibing of a wassail bowl filled with a fragrant concoction of ale, cream, apples, cloves, ginger, and more.[1] Often wassail was consumed among orchards and accompanied by the banging of pots and pans, as a way to ward off evil spirits. Sometimes the wassail bowl was carried from house to house, as neighbors toasted to the coming year.[2] The popularity of the tradition is captured by the once well-known carol "Here We Come a Wassailing"[3]:

Here we come a-wassailing
Among the leaves so green;
Here we come a-wand'ring
So fair to be seen.

Chorus:
Love and joy come to you,
And to you your wassail too;
And God bless you and send you
A Happy New Year
And God send you
    a Happy New Year.

Our wassail cup is made
Of the rosemary tree,
And so is your beer
Of the best barley.
(Chorus)

We are not daily beggars
That beg from door to door;
But we are neighbours' children,
Whom you have seen before.
(Chorus)

Good master and good mistress,
While you're sitting by the fire,
Pray think of us poor children
Who are wandering in the mire.
(Chorus)

We have a little purse
Made of ratching leather skin;
We want some of your small change
To line it well within.
(Chorus)

Call up the butler of this house,
Put on his golden ring.
Let him bring us up a glass of beer,
And better we shall sing.
(Chorus)

Bring us out a table
And spread it with a cloth;
Bring us out a mouldy cheese,
And some of your Christmas loaf.
(Chorus)

God bless the master of this house
Likewise the mistress too,
And all the little children
That round the table go.
(Chorus)

And all your kin and kinsfolk,
That dwell both far and near;
We wish you a Merry Christmas
And a Happy New year.
(Chorus)

FICTIONARY

PLAYERS

4, minimum

ITEMS NEEDED

- Dictionary
- Paper
- Pens or pencils

INSTRUCTIONS

In each round, one player will be the Judge. The Judge reads an obscure word from the dictionary.

The other players write down their made-up definitions of the word.

The Judge reads all the definitions (including the real one) and players vote on which they believe is correct.

Points are awarded by votes and for guessing the correct answer.

WINK MURDER

PLAYERS

6, minimum

ITEMS NEEDED

· None

INSTRUCTIONS

Choose one player to be the Judge.

All players stand in a circle and close their eyes, while the Judge selects a Murderer and a Detective by tapping them on the forehead (one tap for Murderer, two taps for Detective).

Players open their eyes. While the Detective is given three guesses as to the identity of the Murderer, the Murderer may murder other players by winking at them when the Detective is not looking. When murdered, a player must leave the circle.

If the Detective is unsuccessful in identifying the Murderer, he may continue as Detective for a second round. If he successfully identifies the Murderer, the Murderer becomes Detective for the next round.

SQUEAK, PIGGY, SQUEAK

PLAYERS

4–6, minimum

ITEMS NEEDED

· Chairs
· Blindfold
· Pillow

INSTRUCTIONS

Choose a player to be the blindfolded Farmer.

The Farmer sits on a pillow within the circle of other players (or Piggies).

The Farmer spins around several times, then places the pillow in the lap of one of the Piggies, who must then promptly squeal like a pig.

The Farmer guesses the identity of the Piggy.

If he guesses correctly, the Piggy becomes the new Farmer and the games continues.

UP JENKINS

PLAYERS

6–8, minimum

ITEMS NEEDED

- Table
- Chairs
- Coin

INSTRUCTIONS

This game works best at the end of dinner, while everyone is still seated at the table. If necessary, move seats around so that two teams are divided evenly and seated opposite one another at the table.

Choose a Captain for each team.

Team A will pass a coin among themselves, beneath the table (whether or not it is actually being passed is up to them).

Team B tries to guess who has the coin.

If the Captain of Team B shouts "Up Jenkins!" the members of Team A must reveal their closed fists, setting them on the table.

If the Captain of Team B shouts "Down Jenkins!" they must open their fists and slap the table, palms down.

At this point, Team B has one shot at guessing who has the coin. If correct, the coin goes to Team B. If incorrect, it remains with Team A.

Points are awarded whenever a team successfully tricks the other team.

SNAPDRAGON

⊸⊙⁊⊙⊶

hile the precise origins of the parlor game Snapdragon are unclear, we know it emerged sometime in Elizabethan England, was most likely the cause of numerous third-degree burns, and by the nineteenth century had become a time-honored holiday tradition. This dangerous affair, which, by all accounts, seemed to have been invented by bored pyromaniacs, was popular enough to garner mentions by authors such as Shakespeare, Charles Dickens, Lewis Carroll, and Anthony Trollope, and even found its way into Samuel Johnson's 1775 *Dictionary of the English Language.*

The rules of the game, as described by Robert Chambers in his 1869 *Book of Days*, are as follows:

A quantity of raisins are deposited in a large dish or bowl (the broader and shallower this is, the better), and brandy or some other spirit is poured over the fruit and ignited. The bystanders now endeavour, by turns, to grasp a raisin, by plunging their hands through the flames; and as this is somewhat of an arduous feat, requiring both courage and rapidity of action, a considerable amount of laughter and merriment is evoked at the expense of the unsuccessful competitors.

Chambers goes on to suggests that "whilst the sport of Snapdragon is going on, it is usual to extinguish all the lights in the room, so that the lurid glare from the flaming spirits may exercise to the full its weird-like effect. There seems little doubt that in this amusement we retain a trace of the fiery ordeal of the middle ages, and also of the Druidical fire-worship of a still remoter epoch."[4]

As if the delicate business of snatching raisins from a flaming bowl was not sufficient enough for a night's entertainment, players would sometimes attempt to recite the following poem while playing:

Here he comes with flaming bowl,
Don't he mean to take his toll,
Snip! Snap! Dragon!

Take care you don't take too much,
Be not greedy in your clutch,
Snip! Snap! Dragon!

With his blue and lapping tongue
Many of you will be stung,
Snip! Snap! Dragon!

For he snaps at all that comes
Snatching at his feast of plums,
Snip! Snap! Dragon!

But Old Christmas makes him come,
Though he looks so fee! fa! fum!
Snip! Snap! Dragon!

Don't 'ee fear him—be but bold—
Out he goes, his flames are cold,
Snip! Snap! Dragon!

INDEX

ACKNOWLEDGMENTS

Thank you to everyone who had a hand in this book: to Dave Schroeder, who first believed in the vision . . . to Trillia Newbell, Connor Sterchi, Erik Peterson, and everyone else at Moody for their support . . . to Trevin Wax, Carolyn Weber, Dan Wilt, and Jack Mooring for honest feedback along the way . . . to Stephen Crotts, for your beautiful cover design . . . to Kate Healy and Grahame Eke for sharing your family recipes . . . to my wife, Patti, for putting up with the often unpredictable schedule of a freelance author and filmmaker (it's an adventure) . . . to our kids, Audrey, Whitaker, Elam, and Asa, for keeping me young . . . and finally, to Mr. Chesterton himself, without whom, it is safe to say, this book would not exist.

NOTES

INTRODUCTION

1. C. S. Lewis, *Surprised by Joy* (New York: Harcourt Brace Jovanovich, 1984), 181.

2. G. K. Chesterton, *The New Jerusalem* (London: George H. Doran Co., 1921), 90–91.

DAY 1: AN INVITATION TO WALK BACKWARDS THROUGH HISTORY

1. G. K. Chesterton, *The Collected Works of G.K. Chesterton*, vol. 20 (San Francisco: Ignatius Press, 1986), 193. Note: originally from *The New Jerusalem* (1920).

2. G. K. Chesterton, *Tremendous Trifles* (New York: Dodd, Mead & Co., 1920), 245–46.

3. Chesterton, *Collected Works*, vol. 32, 289. Note: originally from an article in *The Illustrated London News*, 1921.

DAY 2: A WARNING TO THOSE IN DANGER OF CELEBRATING CHRISTMAS PREMATURELY

1. G. K. Chesterton, *The Collected Works of G.K. Chesterton*, vol. 27 (San Francisco: Ignatius Press, 1986), 370. Note: originally from an article in *The Illustrated London News*, 1906.

2. Chesterton, *Collected Works*, vol. 36, 394. Note: originally from an article in *The Illustrated London News*, 1933.

3. Chesterton, *Collected Works*, vol. 36, 394. Note: originally from an article in *The Illustrated London News*, 1932–1934.

4. Chesterton, *Collected Works*, vol. 32, 511. Note: originally from an article in *The Illustrated London News*, 1920–1922.

DAY 3: IN REGARD TO CERTAIN OBJECTIONS TO THE CELEBRATION OF CHRISTMAS

1. G. K. Chesterton, *The Man Who Was Orthodox* (London: Dobson Books, Ltd., 1963), 183. Note: originally from an article in *G.K.'s Weekly*, 1936.

2. G. K. Chesterton, *The Collected Works of G.K. Chesterton*, vol. 36 (San Francisco: Ignatius Press, 1986), 193. Note: originally from an article in *The Illustrated London News*, 1933.

3. Tom Holland, "The Myth of 'Pagan' Christmas," December 25, 2021, https://unherd.com/2021/12/the-myth-of-pagan-christmas-2/.

4. Chesterton, *The Man Who Was Orthodox*, 184. Note: originally from an article in *G.K.'s Weekly*, 1936.

5. Chesterton, *Collected Works*, vol. 28, 456. Note: originally from an article in *The Illustrated London News*, 1909.

DAY 4: OF PARADOXES, CELESTIAL LADDERS, AND MOVING WHEELS

1. George Grant and Gregory Wilbur, *Christmas Spirit* (Nashville: Cumberland House Publishing, Inc., 1999), 9. Note: originally from an article in *The Daily News*, 1901.

2. G. K. Chesterton, *The Everlasting Man* (1925; repr., San Francisco: Ignatius Press, 1993), 97.

3. G. K. Chesterton, *Orthodoxy* (1908; repr., New York: Random House, 2001), 24.

4. G. K. Chesterton, *The Collected Works of G.K. Chesterton*, vol. 3 (San Francisco: Ignatius Press, 1986), 332. Note: originally from *The Thing*, 1929.

5. G. K. Chesterton, *The Collected Works of G.K. Chesterton*, vol. 10 (San Francisco: Ignatius Press, 1994), 138.

6. *Merriam-Webster*, s.v. "axis mundi (n.)," https://www.merriam-webster.com/dictionary/axis%20mundi.

7. G. K. Chesterton, *The Everlasting Man* (1925; repr., San Francisco: Ignatius Press, 1993), 184.

8. G. K. Chesterton, *The Collected Works of G.K. Chesterton*, vol. 10 (San Francisco: Ignatius Press, 1994), 139–40.

DAY 5: IN CELEBRATION OF THE UTTER UNSUITABILITY OF CHRISTMAS TO THE MODERN WORLD

1. Marie Smith, ed., *The Spirit of Christmas* (New York: Dodd, Mead & Co., 1985), 79. Note: originally published in *G.K's Weekly*, 1933.

2. G. K. Chesterton, *The Collected Works of G.K. Chesterton*, vol. 35 (San Francisco: Ignatius Press, 1991), 293. Note: originally published in *The Illustrated London News*, 1930.

3. C. S. Lewis, *Surprised by Joy* (New York: Harcourt Brace Jovanovich, 1984), 207.

4. G. K. Chesterton, *The Apostle and the Wild Ducks and Other Essays* (Ann Arbor, MI: The University of Michigan, 1975), 43.

DAY 6: ON CHRISTMAS AS A LITMUS TEST FOR SPIRITUAL BUOYANCY

1. G. K. Chesterton, *The Collected Works of G.K. Chesterton*, vol. 29 (San Francisco: Ignatius Press, 1988), 605. Note: originally from an article in *The Illustrated London News*, 1913.

2. C. S. Lewis, *The Lion, the Witch and the Wardrobe* (New York: HarperCollins, 2000), Dedication.

3. G. K. Chesterton, *The Collected Works of G.K. Chesterton*, vol. 10 (San Francisco: Ignatius Press, 1994), 186. Note: poem written in 1905.

4. G. K. Chesterton, *Orthodoxy* (1908; repr., New York: Random House, 2001), 58.

DAY 7: CONCERNING THE INESCAPABLE FRATERNITY OF THE FAMILY GATHERING

1. Marie Smith, ed., *The Spirit of Christmas* (New York: Dodd, Mead & Co., 1985), 77–78. Note: originally published in *G.K.'s Weekly*, 1933.

2. G. K. Chesterton, *Brave New Family: G.K. Chesterton on Men & Women, Children, Sex, Divorce, Marriage & the Family*, ed. Alvaro de Silva (San Francisco: Ignatius Press, 1990), 259. Note: originally published in *The Thing*, 1929.

3. Chesterton, *Brave New Family*, 260. Note: originally published in *The Thing*, 1929.

DAY 8: AS FOR GAMES AND THE POSSIBLE INVENTION OF NEW ONES

1. G. K. Chesterton, *The Collected Works of G.K. Chesterton*, vol. 3 (San Francisco: Ignatius Press, 1986), 333. Note: also appears in *The Thing*, 1929.

2. Several of these games can be found in the Games & Traditions section of this book.

3. G. K. Chesterton, "Christmas and Sport," in *VII: Journal of the Marion E. Wade Center* 14 (1997): 94, http://www.jstor.org/stable/45296527.

4. G. K. Chesterton, *A Shilling for My Thoughts* (London: Methuen & Co., 1921), 55–56.

5. Chesterton, "Christmas and Sport," *VII* 14, 94.

6. G. K. Chesterton, *The Collected Works of G.K. Chesterton*, vol. 31 (San Francisco: Ignatius Press, 1989), 222. Note: originally published in *The Illustrated London News*, 1917.

7. G. K. Chesterton, *Alarms and Discursions* (London: Methuen & Co., 1910), 22.

8. Chesterton, "Christmas and Sport," *VII* 14, 94.

DAY 9: ON CHRISTMAS AS A DECLARATION OF WAR

1. G. K. Chesterton, *The Everlasting Man* (1925; repr., San Francisco: Ignatius Press, 1993), 180–81.

2. Chesterton, *The Everlasting Man*, 179.

3. C. S. Lewis, *Mere Christianity* (New York: HarperCollins, 2001), 46.

4. Chesterton, *The Everlasting Man*, 180.

5. George MacDonald, *Discovering the Character of God* (Grand Rapids: Bethany House, 1989), 227.

DAY 10: ON CHRISTMAS AS AN ANTIDOTE TO A DISENCHANTED IMAGINATION

1. G. K. Chesterton, *Brave New Family: Family: G.K. Chesterton on Men & Women, Children, Sex, Divorce, Marriage & the Family*, ed. Alvaro de Silva (San Francisco: Ignatius Press, 1990), 263. Note: originally from article in *G.K.'s Weekly*, 1925.

2. Charles Taylor, *A Secular Age* (Cambridge, MS: Harvard University Press, 2007), 34.

3. Taylor, *A Secular Age*, 37–38.

4. Taylor, *A Secular Age*, 3.

5. Taylor, *A Secular Age*, 146.

6. G. K. Chesterton, *The Collected Works of G.K. Chesterton*, vol. 4 (San Francisco: Ignatius Press, 1987), 54. Note: originally published *What's Wrong with the World* (1910).

7. G. K. Chesterton, "The Christmas Story," in *The Speaker*, December 29, 1900.

8. G. K. Chesterton, *Orthodoxy* (1908; repr., New York: Random House, 2001), 63.

9. Chesterton, *Orthodoxy*, 59.

DAY 11: A BRIEF CELEBRATION OF THE BOOMERANG

1. G. K. Chesterton, *The Collected Works of G.K. Chesterton*, vol. 29 (San Francisco: Ignatius Press, 1988), 602. Note: originally published in *The Illustrated London News*, 1913.

2. G. K. Chesterton, *The Collected Works of G.K. Chesterton*, vol. 1 (San Francisco: Ignatius Press, 1986), 88. Note: originally from *Heretics*, 1905.

DAY 12: IN REGARD TO THE ENORMOUS AND OVERWHELMING EVERYTHING

1. G. K. Chesterton, *The Uses of Diversity* (London: Methuen & Co., 1921), 216–17.

2. G. K. Chesterton, *The Everlasting Man* (1925; repr., San Francisco: Ignatius Press, 1993), 34, 45.

3. G. K. Chesterton, "The Theology of Christmas Presents," *The Contemporary Review*, January–June 1910, 69–70.

4. C. S. Lewis, *The Grand Miracle and Other Selected Essays on Theology and Ethics from God in the Dock* (New York: Balantine Books, 1986), 89.

5. A jack-o'-lantern made from a turnip.

6. G. K. Chesterton, *A Miscellany of Men* (London: Dodd, Mead, & Co., 1912), 120.

7. G. K. Chesterton, *The Collected Works of G.K. Chesterton*, vol. 32 (San Francisco: Ignatius Press, 1986), 515. Note: originally published in *The Illustrated London News*, 1922.

8. J. R. R. Tolkien, quoted in Richard Matthews, *Fantasy: The Liberation of Imagination* (Abingdon: Taylor & Francis, 2016), 58.

DAY 13: ON THE JUXTAPOSITION OF FRIGHTFUL WEATHER AND FESTIVE GAIETY

1. G. K. Chesterton, *The New Jerusalem* (London: George H. Doran Co., 1921), 90.

2. William Wordsworth, *The Collected Poems of William Wordsworth* (Hertfordshire: Wordsworth Editions, 1994), 83.

3. Debra Spark, *Curious Attractions: Essays on Writing* (Ann Arbor, MI: University of Michigan Press, 2005), 31. Note: story originally published in 1914.

4. C. S. Lewis, *The Lion, the Witch and the Wardrobe* (New York: HarperCollins, 2000), 19.

5. Victor Hugo, *Les Miserables*, Book 1 (Oxford: Oxford University Press, 1874), 232.

6. Gerard Manley Hopkins, *The Poems of Gerard Manley Hopkins* (London: Oxford University Press, 1967), 67.

7. G. K. Chesterton, *The Collected Works of G.K. Chesterton*, vol. 15 (San Francisco: Ignatius Press, 1989), 133. Note: originally from the book *Charles Dickens*, 1906.

8. G. K. Chesterton, *The Collected Works of G.K. Chesterton*, vol. 11 (San Francisco: Ignatius Press, 1986), 376. Note: originally from the book *George Bernard Shaw*, 1909.

DAY 14: CONCERNING HEARTY BREAKFASTS AND THE PLEASURES OF BEING FLUNG HEADLONG INTO THE SEA

1. G. K. Chesterton, *The Collected Works of G.K. Chesterton*, vol. 28 (San Francisco: Ignatius Press, 1986), 460.

2. Chesterton, *Collected Works*, vol. 27, 370. Note: originally from the book *All Things Considered*, 1908.

3. Chesterton, *Collected Works*, vol. 37, 202–203. Note: originally from an article published in *The Illustrated London News*, 1935.

4. G. K. Chesterton, *All Things Considered* (New York: John Lane Company, 1920), 288.

DAY 15: A WORD ON THE WORD MADE FLESH

1. G. K. Chesterton, *The Collected Works of G.K. Chesterton*, vol. 20 (San Francisco: Ignatius Press, 1986), 76. Note: originally from the book *Christendom in Dublin*, 1932.

2. Timothy Pawl, *In Defense of Conciliar Christology* (Oxford: Oxford University Press, 2016), 30.

3. G. K. Chesterton, *The Everlasting Man* (1925; repr., San Francisco: Ignatius Press, 1993), 179.

4. G. K. Chesterton, *The New Jerusalem* (London: George H. Doran Co., 1921), 175.

DAY 16: ON THE SIGNIFICANCE AND INSIGNIFICANCE OF RITUAL AND ROUTINE

1. G. K. Chesterton, *The Collected Works of G.K. Chesterton*, vol. 37 (San Francisco: Ignatius Press, 1986), 201. Note: originally published in *The Illustrated London News*, 1935.

2. G. K. Chesterton, *All Things Considered* (London: Methuen & Co., 1908), 286.

3. G. K. Chesterton, *Tremendous Trifles* (New York: Dodd, Mead & Co., 1920), 7.

4. Hypocrisy, insincerity.

5. G. K. Chesterton, *Orthodoxy* (1908; repr., New York: Random House, 2001), 63.

DAY 17: A WORD OF GRATITUDE TO SANTA CLAUS

1. Frederick and Mary Ann Brussat, *Spiritual Literacy* (New York: Scribner, 1998), 267. Note: originally appeared in the magazine *Black and White*, 1903.

2. G. K. Chesterton, *Commonweal*, December 20, 1935, 201.

3. G. K. Chesterton, *The Everlasting Man* (1925; repr., San Francisco: Ignatius Press, 1993), 104–105.

4. G. K. Chesterton, *The Collected Works of G.K. Chesterton*, vol. 28 (San Francisco: Ignatius Press, 1986), 249. Note: originally published in *The Illustrated London News*, 1909. Chesterton is intentionally being playful with his language here. The idea of the "gods returning" is an image of the divine returning to a previously disenchanted world.

5. Chesterton, *Collected Works*, vol. 28, 23. Originally published in the article "The Survival of Christmas," *The Illustrated London News*, January 11, 1908.

DAY 18: ON THE ASSOCIATION BETWEEN BABIES AND STAR-SUSTAINING STRENGTH

1. G. K. Chesterton, *The Everlasting Man* (1925; repr., San Francisco: Ignatius Press, 1993), 170–71.

2. G. K. Chesterton, *The Collected Works of G.K. Chesterton*, vol. 1 (San Francisco: Ignatius Press, 1986), 124. Note: originally from the book *Heretics*, 1905.

3. Chesterton, *The Everlasting Man*, 248–49.

DAY 19: IN DEFENSE OF THE MATERIAL SUBSTANCE OF CHRISTMAS PRESENTS

1. G. K. Chesterton, "The Theology of Christmas Presents," *The Contemporary Review*, January–June 1910, 68.

2. From an article in *G.K.'s Weekly* (1931).

DAY 20: WITH RESPECT TO ROT, RIOT, AND RELIGION

1. G. K. Chesterton, *The Collected Works of G.K. Chesterton*, vol. 28 (San Francisco: Ignatius Press, 1986), 24. Note: originally published in *The Illustrated London News*, 1907.

2. G. K. Chesterton, *Orthodoxy* (1908; repr., New York: Random House, 2001), 27.

3. G. K. Chesterton, *The Ballad of the White Horse* (1911; repr., San Francisco: Ignatius Press, 1993), 81.

4. It is possible that this inquiry was posed by a writer for *The Times*. As far as I know, no one has tracked down the column itself, but this story is generally believed to be true.

5. Chesterton, *Orthodoxy*, 170.

DAY 21: AS TO THE UNCOMFORTABLE COMFORT OF CHRISTMAS

1. G. K. Chesterton, *The Collected Works of G.K. Chesterton*, vol. 28 (San Francisco: Ignatius Press, 1986), 25. Note: originally appeared in an article in *The Illustrated London News*, 1907.

2. Chesterton, *Collected Works*, vol. 20, 463. Note: originally from the book *A Short History of England*, 1917.

3. G. K Chesterton, *St. Francis of Assisi* (New York: George H. Doran Company, 1924), 114.

DAY 22: OF BARBARIANS, PHILOSOPHERS, AND A CAVE OF DREAMS

1. G. K. Chesterton, *The Everlasting Man* (1925; repr., San Francisco: Ignatius Press, 1993), 174–75.

2. G. K. Chesterton, *In Defense of Sanity* (San Francisco: Ignatius Press, 2011), 96. Note: originally appeared in the book *The Book of Job*, 1907.

3. Chesterton, *The Everlasting Man*, 110.

4. G. K. Chesterton, *Orthodoxy* (1908; repr., New York: Random House, 2001), 50.

5. C. S. Lewis, *The Collected Works of C.S. Lewis* (Edison, NJ: Inspirational Press, 1996), 343.

DAY 23: TO MARRY, BE MERRY, AND MAKE MERRY

1. G. K. Chesterton, *Brave New Family: G.K. Chesterton on Men & Women, Children, Sex, Divorce, Marriage & the Family*, ed. Alvaro de Silva (San Francisco: Ignatius Press, 1990), 262. Note: originally from an article in *G.K.'s Weekly*, 1925.

2 G. K. Chesterton, *The Collected Works of G.K. Chesterton*, vol. 27 (San Francisco: Ignatius Press, 1986), 103. Note: originally published in *The Illustrated London News*, 1905.

3. G. K. Chesterton, *The Collected Works of G.K. Chesterton*, vol. 4 (San Francisco: Ignatius Press, 1987), 77. Note: originally from the book *What's Wrong with the World*, 1910.

DAY 24: IN REGARD TO THE ANCIENT SYMBOL OF THE FLAME

1. G. K. Chesterton, *The Collected Works of G.K. Chesterton*, vol. 34 (San Francisco: Ignatius Press, 1986), 438–39. Note: originally from an article in *The Illustrated London News*, 1927.

2. Chesterton, *Collected Works*, vol. 30, 17.

3. Kevin Belmonte, *A Year with G. K. Chesterton* (Nashville: Thomas Nelson, 2012), 365. Note: originally from *Generally Speaking*, 1929.

4. Chesterton, *Collected Works*, vol. 30, 124. Note: originally published in *The Illustrated London News*, 1914.

5. Chesterton, *Collected Works*, vol. X (San Francisco: Ignatius Press, 1986), 242.

DAY 25: OF SECRETS, DIVINE CAPS, AND CELESTIAL POST OFFICES

1. *The Contemporary Review* (London: A. Strahan, 1910), 70.

2. G. K. Chesterton, *Orthodoxy* (1908; repr., New York: Random House, 2001), 150.

3. G. K. Chesterton, *The Everlasting Man* (1925; repr., San Francisco: Ignatius Press, 1993), 248.

4. Kevin Belmonte, *A Year with G. K. Chesterton* (Nashville: Thomas Nelson, 2012), 293.

5. G. K. Chesterton, *Orthodoxy* (1908; repr., New York: Random House, 2001), 97.

DAY 26: CONCERNING THE ENDURING FORTITUDE OF CHRISTMAS

1. G. K. Chesterton, *The Collected Works of G.K. Chesterton*, vol. 32 (San Francisco: Ignatius Press, 1986), 290–91. Note: originally from an article in *The Illustrated London News*, 1921.

2. Chesterton, *Collected Works*, vol. 1, 127. Note: originally from the book *Heretics*, 1905.

3. G. K. Chesterton, *The Everlasting Man* (1925; repr., San Francisco: Ignatius Press, 1993), 160.

4. Chesterton, *The Everlasting Man*, 178.

5. Chesterton, *The Everlasting Man*, 250.

6 Chesterton, *Collected Works*, vol. 32, 290. Note: originally from article in *The Illustrated London News*, 1921.

7 Chesterton, *Collected Works*, vol. 28, 23–24. Note: originally published in *The Illustrated London News*, 1908.

DAY 27: WITH RESPECT TO PUDDING, CURRENCY, AND THE BETRAYAL OF CHRISTMAS

1. G. K. Chesterton, *The Collected Works of G.K. Chesterton*, vol. 36 (San Francisco: Ignatius Press, 2011), 395–96. Note: originally from an article in *The Illustrated London News*, 1933.

2. See recipe for Christmas pudding on p. 217.

3. G. K. Chesterton, *The Collected Works of G.K. Chesterton*, vol. 3 (1929; repr., San Francisco: Ignatius Press, 1986), 331. Note: originally from the book *The Thing*, 1929.

4. Chesterton, *Collected Works*, vol. 3, 330.

DAY 28: CONCERNING THE LIBERAL AND CONSERVATIVE BALANCE OF CHRISTMAS

1. G. K. Chesterton, *The Collected Works of G.K. Chesterton*, vol. 33 (San Francisco: Ignatius Press, 1990), 236. Note: originally from an article in *The Illustrated London News*, 1923.

2. G. K. Chesterton, *The Collected Works of G.K. Chesterton*, vol. 29 (San Francisco: Ignatius Press, 1988), 18. Note: originally from an article in *The Illustrated London News*, 1911.

3. From an article in *G.K.'s Weekly*, 1936.

4. From an article in *G.K.'s Weekly*, 1936.

5. G. K. Chesterton, *The Everlasting Man* (1925; repr., San Francisco: Ignatius Press, 1993), 180.

6. G. K. Chesterton, *Orthodoxy* (1908; repr., New York: Random House, 2001), 103.

DAY 29: ON CRACKERS, LOGS, AND THE WINTER BATH OF ECSTASY

1. G. K. Chesterton, *The Collected Works of G.K. Chesterton*, vol. 28 (San Francisco: Ignatius Press, 1986), 251. Note: originally published in *The Illustrated London News*, 1909.

2. Kevin Belmonte, *A Year with G. K. Chesterton* (Nashville: Thomas Nelson, 2012), 1.

3. See Games & Traditions section.

DAY 30: AFTER CHRISTMAS (AN AFTERWORD)

1. G. K. Chesterton, *The Collected Works of G.K. Chesterton*, vol. 37 (San Francisco: Ignatius Press, 1986), 205. Note: originally published in *The Illustrated London News*, 1917.

2. G. K. Chesterton, *The New Jerusalem* (London: George H. Doran Co., 1921), 307.

POEMS

1. G. K. Chesterton, *The Collected Works of G.K. Chesterton*, vol. X (San Francisco: Ignatius Press, 1986), 497.

2. Kevin Belmonte, *Defiant Joy: The Remarkable Life and Impact of G.K. Chesterton* (Nashville: Thomas Nelson, 2011), 37–38. Note: originally published in *The Wild Knight*, 1900.

3. G. K. Chesterton, *The Collected Poems of G.K. Chesterton* (London: Methuen & Co., 1936), 151.

4. Chesterton, *Collected Works*, vol. X, 365.

5. Chesterton, *Collected Works*, vol. X, 100–101.

6. Chesterton, *Collected Works*, vol. X, 181–82.

7. Chesterton, *Collected Works*, vol. X, 186–87.

8. Chesterton, *Collected Works*, vol. X, 139–40.

9. Chesterton, *Collected Works*, vol. X, 148–49.

10. G. K. Chesterton, *The Queen of Seven Swords* (London: Sheed & Ward, 1926), 14.

11. Chesterton, *Collected Works*, vol. X, 137–38.

ESSAYS

1. G. K. Chesterton, *The Collected Works of G.K. Chesterton*, vol. 28 (San Francisco: Ignatius Press, 1986), 21–26.

2. Chesterton, *Collected Works*, vol. 32, 145–49.

3. A character from the play *Douglas* by John Hume.

4. Honoré de Balzac, French novelist and playwright, 1799–1850.

5. Geoffrey Chaucer, English poet and author of *The Canterbury Tales*, c. 1342–1400.

6. Giovanni Boccaccio, Italian Renaissance writer and poet, 1313–1375.

7. A reference to "The Franklin's Tale" from *The Canterbury Tales*.

8. A character in Charles Dickens's *The Pickwick Papers*.

9. Samuel Johnson, the famous "man of letters," 1709–1784.

10. William Cobbett, English journalist and politician, 1763–1835.

11. A pastoral poem by John Milton.

12. A fictional character created by Joseph Addison who "wrote columns" for the magazine *The Spectator*.

13. Chesterton, *Collected Works*, vol. 34, 437–40.

14. The day commemorating the armistice signed by the Allies of World War I and Germany.

15. Chesterton, *Collected Works*, vol. 36, 393–96.

16. G. K. Chesterton, *The Apostle and the Wild Ducks and Other Essays* (Michigan: The University of Michigan, 1975), 45.

SHORT STORIES

1. G. K. Chesterton, *Tremendous Trifles* (New York: Dodd, Mead & Co., 1920), 297–306
2. In this case, Chesterton is referring to democracy in principle.
3. A British writer, politician, and cofounder of the magazine *The Spectator*.
4. A fictional character created by Joseph Addison who "wrote columns" for the magazine *The Spectator*.
5. British playwright and poet.
6. G. K. Chesterton, *The Collected Works of G.K. Chesterton*, vol. XIV (San Francisco: Ignatius Press, 1986), 362–63.
7. A radioactive metal once used in radiotherapy.

RECIPES

1. "The Turkey," in *An Old-Fashioned Christmas*, City Hydro Home Service, 1947, https://www.hydro.mb.ca/corporate/history/an-old-fashioned-christmas.pdf, 1.
2. "Giblet Gravy," in *An Old-Fashioned Christmas*, 1.
3. G. K. Chesterton, "Christmas Thoughts on Vivisection," in *The Collected Works of G.K. Chesterton*, vol. 28 (San Francisco: Ignatius Press, 1987), 17–21. Note: originally from an article in *The Illustrated London News*, 1908.
4. "Hard Sauce," in *An Old-Fashioned Christmas*, 3.
5. See "Christmas Pudding," *Southern Living*, https://www.southernliving.com/recipes/christmas-pudding; Elaine Lemm, "British Christmas Pudding," updated on July 19, 2022, https://www.thespruceeats.com/traditional-christmas-pudding-recipe-435070.
6. Chesterton, *Collected Works*, vol. 27 (San Francisco: Ignatius Press, 1986), 374–75.

GAMES & TRADITIONS

1. See recipe for wassail in the Recipes section.
2. Sally-Anne Huxtable, "Wassailing: Ritual and Revelry," National Trust, https://www.nationaltrust.org.uk/discover/history/art-collections/wassailing-ritual-and-revelry.
3. "Here We Come a Wassailing," Songs for Teaching, https://www.songsforteaching.com/christmas/thewassailsong.php.
4. Hillman's Hyperlinked and Searchable Chambers' Book of Days, http://www.thebookofdays.com/months/dec/24.htm.